Low seams and high visions

Baddesley Ensor of yesteryear

Albert Fretwell

Heart of Albion Press

LOW SEAMS AND HIGH VISTAS
BADDESLEY ENSOR OF YESTERYEAR

Albert Fretwell

ISBN 1 872883 26 5

Printed in England by
D.A.R. Printing (0664) 424785

Heart of Albion Press
2 Cross Hill Close, Wymeswold,
Loughborough, LE12 6UJ

Low seams and high vistas
Baddesley Ensor of yesteryear

The north Warwickshire village of Baddesley Ensor developed around its Common, from which there are wide views in most directions. In recent centuries it became a centre of coal mining, with a number of innovations, including some of the earliest workings of deep seams, which continued to be mined until the recent demise of the last of the pits. Based on a life-long involvement in Baddesley pit and many aspects of village life, this book is a personal account of the village, its common and pits.

Contents

List of illustrations

The author

Albert Fretwell was born in 'Bugs Row', Baddesley, in 1920, the fifth son of a mining family. He was educated at the Church of England School (the 'Infants' School') and the Central School (the 'New School') until leaving at the age of fourteen to start work underground at Baddesley Colliery. He continued his education, firstly at evening classes at Two Gates (walking there and back one night a week for two years until he could afford the bus fare) and then a one-day-a-week course at Nuneaton Technical and Mining School.

His course at Nuneaton was interrupted by the outbreak of the Second World War, when he joined the Royal Naval Air Service, the Fleet Air Arm, as an engine mechanic. He saw service in the North and South Atlantic, round the North Cape, Madagascar, Burma, the Indian Ocean and the Mediterranean. This included Operation Pedestal (the Malta convoys) and North Africa landings. Between tours of active service he served in 787 Squadron, the Naval Air Fighter Development Unit, Z Flight, which perfected the first air-to-ground rocket.

On demobilisation he worked for the Ministry of Fuel and Power's Grendon depot and travelled around the Midlands opencast coal sites, repairing and maintaining the larger diggers, which were leased from the Ministry.

In 1948 he married Kathleen Radford, also from Baddesley, who had often been a classmate at school. They have two sons and a daughter.

When the pits were nationalised Albert returned to Baddesley pit, as a member of the mechanical staff, until ill health caused his retirement in 1980.

When the Baddesley 1st Boy Scout group restarted in 1929, Albert joined as a Wolf Cub. He remained an active member of the group and became Group Scoutmaster, until the headquarters building was sold for development in 1951.

He joined the Baddesley Branch of the British Legion as a Serving Member in June 1940. He held a number of positions culminating in Branch Chairman until poor health led to his resignation in 1989.

Two terms of service on the Parish Council totalled twenty years and involved Albert in many committees such as school management, parks and the village hall.

A lifelong trade unionist and for many years a member of the Baddesley Lodge committee, Albert was Baddesley's representative on the Convalescent Home committee, the Lodge Educational Secretary and Warwickshire Miner's representative for the N.C.L.C. (the nationwide trade union education organisation) until it was taken over by the T.U.C.. He organised many weekly classes and week-end schools.

During the entire period of the village's Allotment Association (subsequently the Horticultural Society) Albert was the Secretary. The Darby and Joan Club requested his assistance as Treasurer in 1974 and he subsequently became Secretary and then Chairman, until ill-health caused his resignation in 1989.

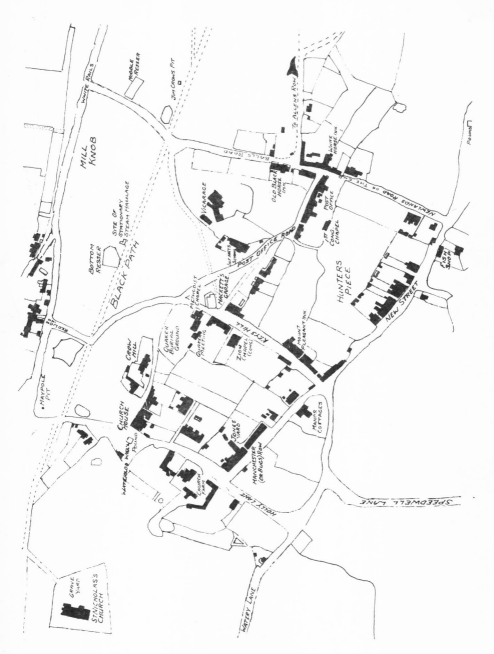

Baddesley Ensor c.1902

Chapter 1

In the beginning

The ground beneath Baddesley

A prehistoric event of interest to Baddesley was Lake Harrison, named after the geologist who first found evidence of it. Prior to the last-but-one Ice Age the whole of the Midlands was drained by what is now the River Soar by way of where Leicester is now. But glacial action during the Ice Age effectively blocked the rivers, with the result that the Midlands were covered by a huge lake, some four hundred square miles in extent, with an island known as the Coventry Island showing above water. It remained so for several hundreds of years.

The interest, as far as Baddesley is concerned, is that the village stands on what was then the northern tip of Coventry Island. The level of the water was 420 feet above present sea level. By glancing at a map, and following the 420 feet [130 metre] contour line, one can get an idea of the extent of the lake. Much of Baddesley was under water, the site of the Liberal Club being the approximate level of the shoreline, while Grendon and Atherstone were hundreds of feet below water.

When the National Coal Board extended the site of the dirt tip in Baxterley Park (paradoxically in Baddesley) they scraped off the top soil to a depth of approximately five feet. They then dug a trench round the perimeter, again approximately five feet deep. Along the northern edge of the site this trench crossed the 420 feet contour line. An examination of the trench showed a layer of silt, two to three inches thick, with a wave beach such as one would expect to find at a shoreline. This was at a depth of approximately nine to ten feet below ground level.

Ancient artefacts

Quite a number of ancient artefacts have been found in the parish, but one wonders how many more would have been found had the parish not have been well and truly turned-over by various industrial activities.

The parish is roughly pear-shaped, lying on a north-south axis, with the stalk end of the pear to the south. It is roughly bisected by the Kingsbury Mineral Spur railway, which created a trauma of upheaval, digging cuttings and building enbankments. The coal seams run down the eastern edge of the parish, so that east of the railway the land has been largely disturbed by pits and opencast coal sites. A seam of spirorbic limestone runs down the western edge of the parish, so that side of the parish has been turned over in the extraction of lime. In all, quite a proportion of the parish has been lost as far as finding history on the ground is concerned. Added to this, the use since the Second World War of the deeper, tractor-drawn plough has led to the last vestiges of many historical landmarks being lost. For instance the last traces of the ha-ha (a form of deer trap) and of the common fields all disappeared in the last few years.

Further, miles and miles of hedgerows, with their intermittent broad leafed trees, have been grubbed out. There is a formula, based on counting the number of different species of shrubs and plants in a hedgerow, by which one can estimate how many centuries old a hedgerow is. But we can never estimate the age of hedgrows that have been taken out.

Despite all these activities a surprising number of artefacts have been found, ranging from flint scrapers from the Neolithic to the Bronze Ages. They were mainly scattered all over the sloping field known popularly as Dickie's Hill. After many years of ploughing they could have slid down even from the top of the hill.

Roman pot sherds have been found in the fields on the opposite side of Lower House Lane, in the fields adjacent to the Lower House Farm (commonly known today as the Skin Farm). One is of Samian ware, a high quality Roman pottery, comparable with modern china ware.

One interesting find was made at Hill Top. A quite insignificant-looking piece of sandstone, approximately two inches square, had unusual markings on it. Fortunately the finder found it of interest and reported it. When sent to the British Museum in London it was identified as an Iron Age brooch mould. An object as small as this is portable and may have been left either by a resident or passer-by, but at the very least it shows that someone was around Hill Top, nearly 1,000 years BC.

Baedes-lei or Bedesley

Around 410 AD, after four centuries of occupying Britain, the Roman legions were withdrawn. Four centuries during which the Welsh-speaking inhabitants of the country, the Britons, were not permitted to bear arms, leaving behind a country ill-equipped to defend itself - a situation soon to be exploited by the war-like Germanic tribes: the Angles, the Saxons and the Jutes, followed by the Vikings. At that time North Warwickshire was covered by the Forest of Arden, with occasional clearings, called 'lei's' or 'ley's', being farmed by the Britons. Quite a few of these leys are commemorated today in the names of villages that have grown on their sites e.g. Ansley, Bentley and Hurley to mention a few. Or, in our case, Baddesley.

The colonisation of Warwickshire by the Germanic tribes began around 640 with the Angles travelling westward from the Wash, and the Saxons travelling northward up the Avon valley, meeting somewhere around Warwick. They travelled in organised groups each with a leader. So that, when they settled, it was in an organised manner, with their dwellings around or adjacent to their leader's dwelling. They seem to have shown little or no interest in North Warwickshire, with its hilly, wooded terrain and shallow top-soil. Instead, they went for the more readily-cultivated, fertile Feldon country of south Warwickshire.

The second wave of colonisation came some thirty to forty years later, by way of the tributaries of the river Trent. It consisted mainly of family groups, probably one man and his family together with the family's slave or slaves, who took over the lei's previously farmed by the Britons, driving out or possibly enslaving the Britons. Their settlements tended to be more fragmented, and they would appear to have been more of an independent nature, a trait they have retained ever since, often being referred to as 'bloody minded'. One of the most common Germanic family names was Bæde, the 'a' and the 'e' being joined together to form one letter, a letter long since fallen into disuse, and today the name would be spelt Bede, as is the name of the venerable Bede, the Anglo-Saxon monk and writer.

In the time of King Edward the Confessor a Saxon knight, Britric, held the manor from the Saxon Earl of Warwick, Turchil, and still did, twenty years after the Norman Conquest, at the time of William I's great Domesday survey. In this the manor is referred to as 'Bedeslei'. It reads: 'from T[urchil], [King]

William holds Bedeslei. There are three villeins, five bordars, two serfs and one Knight [probably Britric], with arable land for one plough. There is woodland one and a half leagues long and half a league broad. It was and is worth ten shillings. Of the estate [King] William seized upon [*præoccupavit*], a fifth part to the wrong of Super W regen [King William]; and a certain Britric who used to hold it T.R.E. [in King Edward the Confessor's time] dwells there. The other part of the estate [*aliam terram*] Archil and Cerret, Turchil's men hold.'

Bedeslei Ednesoure

The Normans came to Britain not as settlers but as over-lords and lords, to collect taxes and build castles in strategic positions. Their impact on the ordinary people was minimal, taxes were taxes whether they were collected by Saxons or Normans, and serfdom was serfdom no matter who was the lord. King William divided the country up, county by county, between the Norman counts who had supported him in his conquest; they in turn shared out the manors between their own knights.

Unlike other Saxon lords and overlords Britric and Turchil were allowed to hold their lands until 1086, probably until Turchil had completed building Warwick Castle for the Normans. In 1086 the Norman Henry de Beaumont was made Earl of Warwick by William II, and Britric lost his lordship. He proved to be the last resident Lord of the Manor of Baddesley for over five hundred years. Soon after it was taken over by the Norman Earl, the manor of Baddesley was given to the monks of Garendon in Leicstershire. It was taken back later on the payment of ten marks in silver, and half a knight's fee, to be paid from the lands the Earl held at Ibstock. (A knight's fee was the amount of land for which the services of a knight were accorded, the knight to serve in the king's army as and when required, together with his retainers. Quite often the term referred to the money to pay for such services.)

The manor was handed to the Sauvage family. Then, in the absence of one definite heir, the lordship of the manor passed acrimoniously from one member of the Norman family to another branch of the same family - the Sauvages to the Harecourts then back to the Sauvages, then by way of a female heir of the Sauvages to Thomas de Ednesoure. None of these families resided in Baddesley. The de Ednesoures held Pooley and Baginton in Warwickshire, in addition to manors in other counties, principally Derbyshire. Baddesley was let to various sub-tenants as a source of income.

4

There were, and still are, two Baddesley's in Warwickshire. During the lordship of Thomas de Ednesoure the name of their lords was affixed to differentiate them. The name of de Clinton was added to one and that of de Ednesoure to the other. Over the years this has corrupted to Ensor and so we have Baddesley Ensor.

The Hemlingford Hundred

The history of Warwickshire began in the tenth century. But the name *Wærincwicsir* is not recorded before 1016. At first, the county was the area which supported the *burh* or fortress which Lady Æthelflæd of the Mercians had built in 914 as a defence against the Danes. Probably around that time the county was divided up into ten-or-so units known as 'Hundreds' - so-named because each contained approximately one hundred demenses. Each hundred dealt with its own local finance and justice.

At the time of the Domesday Survey, Baddesley was in the Colshelle Hundred which met at Coleshill. But in the Pipe Roll of the eighth year of the reign of Henry II, 1161-62, it was named as the Hemlingford Hundred. Around this time several of the smaller hundreds joined into four larger divisions - the Barlichway, the Kineton, the Knightlow and the Hemlingford Hundreds. Except for Barlichway, these were known as 'ship sokes' and probably had to provide the King with a ship each, for the purpose of national defence.

The hundred system used to be attributed to Alfred the Great but was most likely started in the West Saxon kingdom, and brought to the Midlands in the tenth century, when they came under the rule of Alfred's descendants. It was not only a fiscal unit with a reeve (later to become a bailiff) who served as a royal agent, but also a judicial unit with a court and a police force. It also served as a unit for home defence until the war with Napoleon.

The area covered by the Hemlingford Hundred was the whole of the north and north-western quarter of Warwickshire, including the Tamworth, Atherstone and Nuneaton districts. The original meeting place - Hemlingford near Kingsbury - has virtually disappeared, with Hemlingford bridge destroyed. More recently the garden centre bearing the name has closed. It seems strange that the centre of the Hundred has disappeared, while a small village in the Hundred has grown into the second-largest city in the country - Birmingham.

The reason for moving from Coleshill was probably that Hemlingford was nearer to Kingsbury, at that time the home of the Ardens, the sheriffs of the county. The hundred court leet (three-weekly court) was always held in the court room of Kingsbury Hall. On the annual meetings, held on Martinmas

Day, the warth money was paid by the various towns in the hundred to meet the costs of the castle guard.

Hemlingford hundred belonged to the monarch until Queen Elizabeth I granted it to the Cave family. It passed by marriage to the Aston family, who held it until around 1800 when they sold it to Sir Robert Peel, founder of the police force, who lived at Drayton Manor. He is said to have received £100 a year from the hundred. By this time the hundred had ceased to play any part in the administration of the county. The leet court still met and dealt with cases of debt, trover (wrongful withholding of goods) and of disputes under £40. The proceedings were far too cumbrous and costly for the small sums involved. There was a public outcry after a particularly harrowing case when a man was dispossessed because he owed for two glasses of beer which led to a Bill to increase the powers of the recently established county courts. The Hemlingford hundred court was abolished in 1852.

A point of interest. During Sir Willoughby Aston's lordship, two halfpenny coins were issued by his bailiff, for use in the hundred. One had on the obverse side a head, full face, with the legend 'EDWARD TAYLOR ****BYLIFE', and on the reverse '**** HIS HALFPENNY * 1668'.

Lordship of the Manor

When Simon de Montfort, Earl of Leicester, rebelled against King Henry III, Thomas de Ednesoure joined him. When, in 1265, the revolt was put down and de Montfort killed at the battle of Evesham, Thomas was stripped of his lands, which passed to the Marmions of Tamworth. However, Thomas appealed against the decision to strip him of his lands, by virtue of a cup presented to his grandmother, Leticia de Arden, by Henry II, when she was Henry's concubine. He was probably claiming to be of royal blood, albeit on the wrong side of the blanket. His appeal was successful and, by a decree known as the Dictum de Kenilworth, he had his lands restored, together with other privileges.

Apparently as amends Thomas gave to the monks of Stoneleigh his lands at Hill Wooton, and to the nuns of Polesworth he gave a piece of land 125 feet long by 61 feet broad, containing the chapel dedicated to Saint Nicholas, in his manor of Baddesley. To Alan, the vicar at Baddesley, he bestowed a tenement, as his forefathers had to previous vicars. It was for these good works that he was styled a knight. At the time of his death, in 1285, the manor of Baddesley consisted of one capital messuage, half a water mill and two virgates of demesne, valued at 40 shillings yearly.

6

Thomas died without issue and left a third of his manor to his widow Alice in dower, his heirs being his sisters Amice and Joan, and Joan's grandson Richard de Herthull who, at the time, was eighteen years of age and a ward of the King. Once again, in the absence of one definite Lord of the Manor, there was again a period of internecine squabbling between relatives. At one time one of them held the manor by fealty and the service of a pair of gilt spurs valued 6d (2.5p). Another held it on a rent of a pair of white silk gloves paid annually.

The manor stayed with the Herthull family and, prior to his death in 1389, Richard de Herthull made various settlements of the manor. But in 1404 a Laurence Allesthorpe and others claimed that they were 'violently dispossessed' by Sir John Cockayn, Richard's grandson, and a writ was issued for Sir John to explain his actions. He was a little premature as, on the death of his mother in 1417, all rights to the manor were released to him. The Cockayn family held the lordship of the manor until 1603. All this time they resided at Pooley Hall.

There was a break when the Earl of Warwick (the Kingmaker) was killed at the battle of Barnet. His lands were confiscated and the manor of Baddesley was held by the King, as was his manor at Hinckley. It was at this time that the Baddesley Close was enclosed by a fence and embankment, or 'ha-ha'.

Ploughing up old pottery

Finding pot sherds and such like is most common on ploughed land, especially freshly ploughed land. Pasture land rarely reveals anything, so that a mixture of ploughed and pasture land gives a distorted picture. The ages-old practice of throwing broken pots onto the midden, then scattering the sherds during muck spreading, can distort the suggestions of early settlement.

In the Purgatory (the small triangular field, which unfortunately had its hedgerow grubbed out making it one with one with the larger field, between the brook and the Lower House Lane) and further along this larger field, in the vicinity of the Bull's Head, post-mediaeval roof tiles have been found. This is hardly surprising as on a map, undated but apparently of the early 1700s and titled 'Holdings in Badgely', buildings are shown at the Bull's Head. One, a largish 'L'-shaped house, is marked as 'Home'.

Many medieaval pot sherds have been found on 'Dickies Hill' (incidentally the name of that field is Upper Keys Close), on the Purgatory and on the fields now one with the Purgatory (that is, Church Close and Pool Close). Such finds have also been made on the other side of the Lower House

Lane, as far as the parish boundary, which is only a couple of hundred yards short of Wood End and Freasley.

Unfortunately the area with the greatest potential, around the old church and the churchyard, is overgrown with trees and shrubs, and so is a non-starter as far as finding artefacts is concerned. This area has never been ploughed to bring to the surface anything of interest.

Baddesley Close

Ploughing, especially the ploughing done in the last half century with deeper, tractor-drawn ploughs, has obliterated many landmarks, such as the bank surrounding Baddesley Close. Such bank and ditches are generally known as a 'park pale', but locally as the 'ha-ha'. Baddesley Close was, therefore, a

Henry's fish and chip shop, New Street. One of the best-remembered parts of the old village. The two cottages opposite were demolished for road widening in 1937.

piece of land surrounded by a bank, with a fence at the top of the bank. A deer could leap over the fence to get in, but could not run up the bank from the ditch to leap over the fence to get out.

Baddesley Close was marked on all maps of any age and lay astride Rotherhams Hill and on down to the brook the other side of the railway line. It was probably the pasture inclosed in 1481 by special permission from the king. The ha-ha was probably put in at that time.

The railway was put across Baddesley Close in 1879, and the first ten council houses were built there in 1921. The portion of the bank between the railway and the stream was ploughed out in 1952, when that field was put to the plough for the first time. Walnut Croft, built in Henry 'Wakey's' field, obliterated that portion of the bank. Henry 'Wakey' Albrighton (called a 'Wakey' Albrighton, because he was not a 'Cob' Albrighton, 'Kitty' Albrighton, 'Toddy' Albrighton or a 'Stumpy' Albrighton nor yet a 'Dessy' Albrighton) is well-remembered for his 'Henry's Up-to-Date Fish and Chip Saloon'.

The last traces of the ha-ha were obliterated recently, when the owners of No.'s 1 and 2 Rotherhams Hill altered their gardens to include garages.

Until 1984, the last traces of Baddesley's common fields could be discerned, in the fields between the railway line and the old Ivy House, but since then this land has been put to the plough and all traces have vanished.

The Old Hall

Sir John Cockayne's holdings were restored to the family, as we find that they rebuilt Pooley Hall in 1507, using brick. This was probably the first brick building in Warwickshire. When the Romans left the country, the art of brickmaking went with them and it was not until the Flemish brickmakers re-introduced the art, in the fifteenth century, that bricks were used again in this country; any used in the interim were ones salvaged from old Roman buildings.

One interesting point. The wainscotting in Pooley Hall is of black oak, the same wood as in the so-called Latimer's pulpit from Baddesley's old church. What is more, the carving on the wainscotting is very similar to the carving on the pulpit. One wonders whether the same craftsmen were responsible for both. After all, the Cockaynes were the Lords of Baddesley manor and they are of the same period.

The Lord owned everything in the manor, and held his own manorial court where everything happening in the manor was dealt with. They even

*Baddesley Old Hall as enlarged by Francis Levinge when he
bought the Lordship of the Manor from the Cockaynes in 1603.*

passed their own bye-laws, know as 'pains' and set penalties for contravening
them, known as the manorial 'Pains and Penalties'. The last 'Pains and
Penalties' were issued in 1850.

Edward Cockayne sold the manor and some farms in 1603. The manor
went to Francis Levinge, who is recorded as dealing with a moiety of the
manor in 1599. He was still the Lord of the Manor at the time of his death in
1621. At that time the manor included a *messuage* (a house with its
outbuildings), 16 cottages, a water mill and a windmill. The watermill was
probably Roland's mill, shown on early maps on the Penmire brook, near the
Watling Street, opposite the Coppice restaurant.

The *messuage* undoubtedly was the old Baddesley Hall, formerly built of
sandstone but, around the time of the sale of the manor, it was greatly enlarged
in brick, as befitted a Lord of the Manor's house. One interesting feature was
the massive brick chimney built on to the western end, the sandstone part of
the building, with several mini roofs connecting it to the building itself.

It is said that the skyline of Britain changed dramatically in or around the
year 1600 - in the same way that it changed in 1950, with the introduction of
the television dipole aerials. In 1600 it was the introduction of chimneys. Prior

10

to that a hole in the roof had sufficed. Any old house with an awkward looking chimney attached, is probably a pre-1600 house with the chimney added around that time.

When the Old Hall ceased to be used as a manor house it was converted into four cottages, and continued to be used as such until well after the World War II, until being demolished in the 1950s. Recently I was shown a pre-war tenancy contract for one of the cottages, the rent being 2s 9d (14p) per week.

The lordship of the manor stayed with the Leving family into the eighteenth century. Thomas Leving, who inherited the manor from his father Francis, was escheator for the counties of Warwickshire and Leicestershire. Letters written by him in Baddesley in the 1640s are available. In 1666 a Francis Leving, presumably the grandson of the aforementioned Francis, was dealing with the manor and, when in 1675 Thomas died, the manor passed to the younger Francis.

There was at least one other landowner in the manor at this time, as we find that George Abbot (the Roundhead) was living at Lower House (the Old Ivy House) when he died in 1649. He left a number of bequests to be paid for out of his lands in Baddesley. He was a Member of Parliament for Tamworth and it has been alleged that he used his position as an MP to further his activities in enclosures. But more of him elsewhere.

Dugdales in Baddesley.

With the ending of the Levings' hold on the lordship, the manor would seem to have been divided up. The advowson (the right to appoint a parish vicar) was in the gift of the Lord of the Manor in 1736. But in 1779 a twelfth of the manor was the object of a fine levied between a Thomas Barber, John Warr and others. And the year before that William Harrison and his wife conveyed nine-sixteenths of the manor to Richard Geast. This introduced the Dugdales to the manor.

In 1625 Sir William Dugdale (the antiquarian's father) bought Blythe End, a manor near Coleshill, from Sir Walter Aston. It is said that Sir William completed his book *Antiquities of Warwickshire* there. The manor of Blythe stayed with the Dugdales until 1749 when Sir John (the author's grandson) died leaving no male heir, the estate passing to Richard Geast, son of Sir John's sister Jane, who had married Richard Geast senior of Handsworth. The title was of course extinguished.

Richard Geast junior married Penelope Bate Stratford, daughter and co-heir of Francis Stratford of Merevale. When he inherited the Dugdale

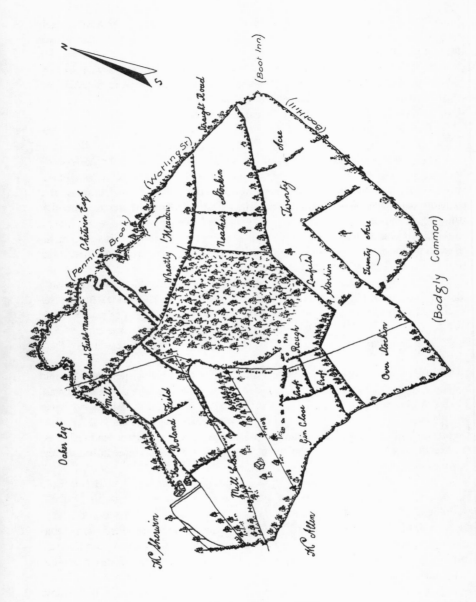

Baddesley Ensor c.1760

estates he changed his name to Dugdale. So, in addition to being the major Lord of the Manor of Baddesley, he also had Merevale and Blythe. They have since acquired the lordship of several other adjacent manors also. However it was always 'Mr Dugdale', until William Francis Stratford Dugdale was made a baronet around 1937. On his death the title passed to the present Sir William who, incidentally, resides at Blythe Hall.

Current Lords of the Manor

Today the present Sir William is the major Lord of the Manor, the rest of the lordship was held by Mr Joseph Thompson, who used to farm Baddesley Farm, on the Lower House Lane. When Mr Thompson died his portion of the lordship was shared between his two daughters, one of whom married Dr Whiteside, who may be remembered for his involvement with the St John's Ambulance Brigade, and with the British Legion (now the Royal British Legion). The standard bearers of the R.B.L branches in Group 5, the North Warwickshire Group, still compete annually for the Dr Whiteside Cup.

The other daughter married Mr Paul, a solicitor who lived at Wilnecote. He was equally well-known as the Commissioner of the Tamworth Boy Scout Association. After their deaths, it would seem that their portions of the lordship were shared among their families. So that we have Sir William, the major lord, and the rest of the lordship shared among members of the Whiteside and Paul families.

When Farmer Thompson was alive he regularly walked round the common and any fence or such like encroaching on the common was removed very smartly. One gentleman who had bought a bit of the common, to have access to his home, had his attempts to fence thwarted several times.

Lordship of the manor normally means very little today. But Baddesley is an exception. Their lordships still own the part of the manor that has never been sold, the common.

The Common

Most other local commons have been either sold or enclosed - or both. For instance, Grendon Common was sold off when the Chetwynd estate was sold up in 1911. It is now completely built up and no longer exists. Older Baddesley residents are infuriated that the Ordnance Survey maps label part of Baddesley Common as Grendon Common. As a result, houses in Baddesley are paradoxically addressed as being on Grendon Common. In fact, Grendon

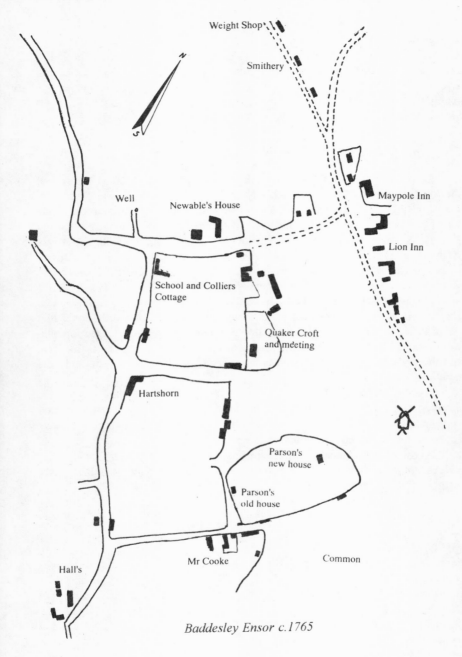

Weight Shop

Smithery

Well

Newable's House

Maypole Inn

Lion Inn

School and Colliers
Cottage

Quaker Croft
and meeting

Hartshorn

Parson's
new house

Parson's
old house

Hall's

Mr Cooke

Common

Baddesley Ensor c.1765

14

Allen's Row, a row of cottages on Baddesley Common.
The end two were demolished by a bomb on May 6th 1942.

Common used to occupy the block of land from the Riddings Lane (Kingy's Lane) to Cookes Lane and the Brickle Pits, the rear of the Maypole Inn, and from Grendon Wood to the boundary of St Nicholas Estate and lower Boot Hill.

Baxterley Common was the subject of the last Enclosure Act in Warwickshire when both of the Baxterley Commons - the Greater Common, on which the pit stood, and the Lesser Common or Wigston Hill Common - were enclosed in 1868. These no longer exist either.

In 1968 the Parish Council applied to have the Baddesley common registered as a common, as they thought that they owned a common right. Early this century Mr 'Tommy' Slack organised a collection in the village and bought Mr Jim Fretwell's common right. This was presented to the Parish Council to safeguard the future of the common. The action was accepted as a *fait accompli* and nothing was done on the common without the Parish Council's consent. A couple of years before the registration hearing the solicitors of the their lordships bowled a 'googly'. They informed the Parish Council that the common rights were attached to property and as they, the Parish Council, did not own the property to which the common right was attached, their common right was invalid. A worthless piece of paper.

Several of the older properties in the parish have common rights attached to them. But no-one knew how many or which ones Even the owners did not realise that they held common rights, they were merely written into the

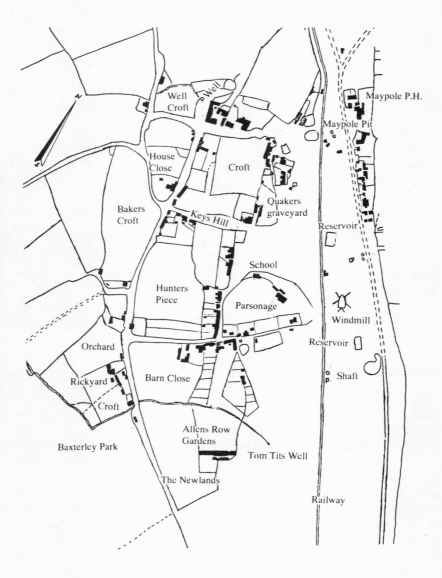

Baddesley Ensor c.1840

property deeds. The Parish Council approached every likely property owner. At the same time they applied for registration, as the registration of just one commoner's rights would have made the common safe as a common forever. Either through ignorance, indifference or just bloody mindedness no one would even admit to owning commoner's rights. Even one pillar of the community, who had previously boasted of owning one, changed his tune. Later, when the property in question was sold, the common right was found among the deeds. Several other new property owners have found rights written into their deeds. These are now probably extinguished for want of registration.

It was nearly twenty years after the application for registration was made before the hearing was heard. At the time of the application their lordships agreed to the application provided that the Parish Council omitted certain parts from the application. These were, the Old Zach's, that is, the piece alongside the rear of Manor Close; the 'Londin Gates' (Landing Gates), where the Speedwell Pit Landsale used to stand opposite No. 42 Hill Top; and the portion that the Church of England or Infants' School was built on. This was acceded to. But by adroit legal footwork their lordships' solicitors caught the Parish Council wrong footed. So that, although the common was registered as a common (and still is) the Parish Council had to pay the costs of the hearing. However the North Warwickshire Borough Council helped to pay them.

There is a possibility that at some time in the future their lordships could apply to have the common de-registered. There are a good few building plots on the 86 acres of the common.

Pinfolds or Penfolds

There were two 'penfolds' or cattle pounds - or as they were known in Baddesley - 'pinfolds'. Both were of a heavy corrugated zinc sheet construction, one opposite the Church House, the other a more robust affair adjacent to the Parkside Bridge. On the map previously referred to, titled 'Holdings in Baddesley', the field on which the Parkside Bridge was built is labelled 'Penfold'. This was part of the croft inundated by the railway embankment and used as a residence by the contractor, John Perkins. One can only assume that Mr Perkins, having buried a good proportion of the Penfold field, had to replace it with an alternative.

The penfold was used to pen cattle, horses or cows, found grazing on the common, but belonging to people who did not hold either a common right or a grazing right. The animals were confined until their owner paid a fine. Common rights have been mentioned before, but in the case of a grazing right,

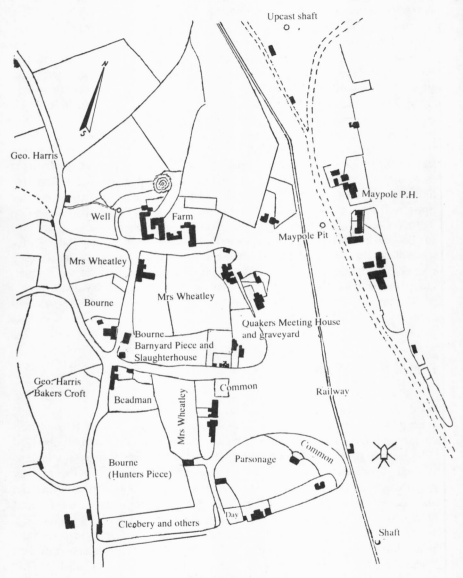

Upcast shaft

Geo. Harris

Well   Farm

Mrs Wheatley

Bourne   Mrs Wheatley

Maypole P.H.

Maypole Pit

Quakers Meeting House
and graveyard

Bourne
Barnyard Piece and
Slaughterhouse

Geo. Harris
Bakers Croft

Beadman   Common

Mrs Wheatley   Railway

Bourne
(Hunters Piece)   Parsonage   Common

Day   Shaft

Cleobery and others

Baddesley Ensor c.1850

The embankment and bridge on the site of a smallholding
occupied by John Perkins while the line was being built.
The pinfold was demolished in the 1930s.

a horse owner paid the Lords of the Manor ten shillings [50p] a year for the right to let his horse graze on the common.

The last 'Penner' or 'Pinner' was Mr Perce Wood, who farmed the Hall Farm, to which the residue of the inundated croft was added. The Bentley pinfold is still standing, a derelict sandstone construction at the junction of the Bentley road and the Coleshill to Atherstone road.

Colliery Waste Tips

A great obliterator of ancient landmarks in the parish are the colliery spoil banks, or dirt mounds, although the size of the spoil banks has increased tremendously since pit cages were introduced around 1850. Prior to that, when buckets or 'hoppits' were wound up and down, the coal had to be transhipped from tubs or trams to the hoppits at the shaft bottom, and any dirt in the tubs was sent back 'inbye' (towards the coal face). So, in the pre-cage pits, the spoilbanks consisted mainly of the debris from the shaft sinking. With the introduction of the cages the tubs were sent straight up the shaft before being emptied, bringing any dirt to the surface.

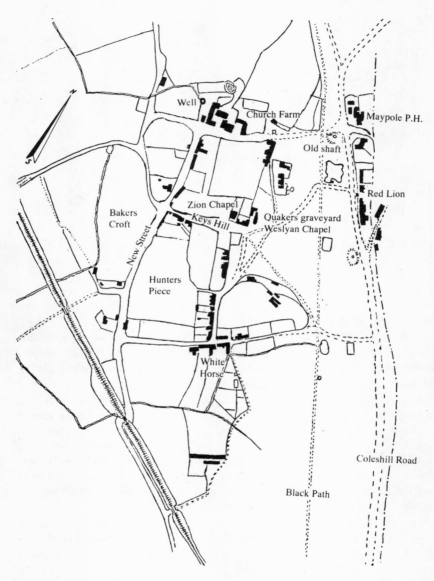

Well

Church Farm

Maypole P.H.

Old shaft

Red Lion

Bakers
Croft

Zion Chapel

Keys Hill

Quakers graveyard

Weslyan Chapel

New Street

Hunters
Piece

White
Horse

Coleshill Road

Black Path

Baddesley Ensor c.1887

An impression of Baxterley Hall, viewed from the Park.
The Hall burned down last century.

The biggest dirt mounds were those at the last Baddesley Pit, erstwhile the 'Stratford Pits', that in its time had three spoil banks. The original one, on the site later occupied by the washery, was removed to facilitate the installation of various surface plant. In the 1920s a bridge was put over the Coleshill Road, over which the dirt taken and was tipped on the Merevale side. The whole of the time that dirt was being tipped there the mound was on fire, having ignited by spontaneous combustion. The dust and fumes penetrated everywhere, including the homes of people living nearby - the local residents were continually complaining. One can still see today that it completely burned through, the claystone or 'clot' (as it is locally known) having been baked to form a pink terracotta shale, known as 'byard', in the same way that unglazed clayware, when fired, produces pink terracotta ware.

By 1953 the tip on the Merevale site had reached its limits (the boundary of what used to be Baxterley common) and the National Coal Board were refused an extension on to the farm land adjacent, on the grounds that it was a potential granite quarry. In 1953 the NCB sought permission to tip on the

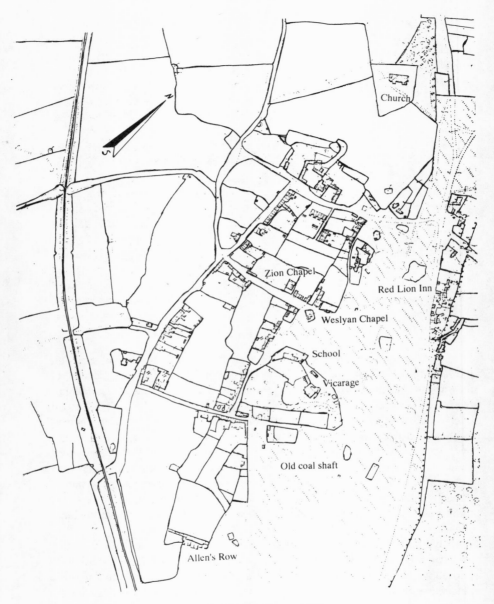

Baddesley Ensor 1903

Baxterley Park for three years, this being the length of time they estimated it would take to clear the Merevale site, before tipping was to recommence there.

NCB gained permission and started tipping in the Baxterley Park in August 1956. They were still tipping there when the pit closed in early 1989, and the mound on the Merevale site has not been cleared yet. The original agreement required NCB to plant a screen of trees, to prevent the proposed mound being an eyesore to the village. These were planted - and soon after they proceeded to tear the trees out.

This time the tipping was layered to prevent spontaneous combustion. Although an aerial ropeway was used in the early days, this was frought with problems so was replaced by dumper trucks.

Paradoxically, most of the Baxterley Park is in Baddesley, the parish boundary crossing the park, in fact the whole of the portion of the park tipped on is in Baddesley. So that the pit was paying rates to Baxterley and tipping its waste in Baddesley who got nothing. It was the park of the Baxterley Hall which burned down some time after 1840. All that is left is the well-preserved ice house, known locally as 'The House Underground'. Most large country houses had ice houses, they performed the function of a refrigerator. Sited usually in a wood or spinney, so that they were in the shade, and underground to make them even cooler, ice packed in straw was put into them in the winter. The invention of the refrigerator spelt their death knell.

New Street near the Post Office.

Chapter 2

Churches and Chapels

Baddesley Old Church

The old church was dedicated to St Nicholas and not, as some would have it, to St Michael. The church at Baddesley Clinton is dedicated to St Michael and this has led to some confusion. *White's Gazeteer* of last century incorrectly states that Baddesley Ensor church was dedicated to St Michael.

The old church was sited some distance outside the village, one of the reasons for its undoing. It was separated from the Old Hall by a tract of land, now under cultivation, but pre-war known as Low Common. Low Common was cleared and put to the plough as a wartime measure by the Warwickshire Agricultural Committee, and has been cultivated ever since. But pre-war it was grazed by cattle and was a popular picnic area for villagers, especially the old pit spoil heap known as the Bunny Bank. Low Common was also popular as a meeting for place for the youths and girls of Baddesley and Dordon, being almost equidistant from the two villages, especially on summer Sunday afternoons.

Ploughing Low Common had an adverse effect on the old church's graveyard. The cattle grazing Low Common also grazed the old churchyard between the gravestones and, despite the cowpats, kept the churchyard clear. Cultivation of Low Common prevented cattle grazing and the churchyard soon became an impenetrable mass of hawthorn, silverbirch and ferns. The Parish Council had it cleared in 1988 by a Manpower Services Youth scheme but it is rapidly deteriorating again.

No one knows when the old church was built or by whom. It was a two-cell building, built in the Romanesque or (as it is known in Britain) the Norman style. Its best feature was probably the red sandstone chevron-moulded Norman doorway. There are around the country several other near-identical

Above: *The old Norman St Nicholas church, demolished around 1850.*
Below: *The old church font, now in Attleborough churchyard.*

churches, except that they do not have a tower. One wonders whether the tower was added to accommodate the solitary bell. This bell, weighing approximately one and a half hundredweights was cast in 1706, and was inscribed RIDE*GOODE*CHURCH*WARDING*****1706****. It was cast

by Joseph Smith of Edgbaston, and presumably hung in the church around that time.

The font was a triangular one of carved sandstone, contemporary with the church. The base had carved recessed arches while the lip was chevron-moulded. The three sides were inscribed 'The Father', 'The Son' and 'The Holy Spirit', in Latin. The window arches were typical Norman designs, all being chevron moulded.

26

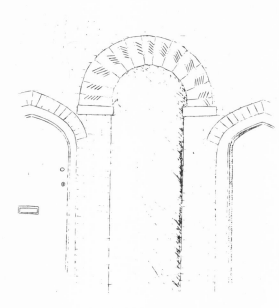

Above: *The doorway of the old St Nicholas church, now set in the north of St Mary's, Atherstone.*

Left: *A chevron-moulded Norman window arch from the old church, set over an entry in a row of cottages known as the Gullet.*

27

The black oak pulpit from the old church, known as the Latimer Pulpit, as it was when installed in the Quaker Meeting House by the Methodists around 1850.

Chevron or 'zig zag' moulding was one of the more popular of the Norman decorative themes. The pulpit was a black oak one of around 1500, five-sided with a large sounding board. Locally it acquired the name 'Latimers Pulpit', but more of this later.

There is very little of the fabric of the church left, after having been ruthlessly plundered for its masonry, as will be related later. Just a bit of the eastern wall is still in situ - a few stones of the bottom course, alongside the overgrown remains of a sunken lane.

In pre-photography 1820, Lord Aylesbury had drawings made of all the local churches. It is from the drawing in his collection that we know what the old church looked like. Fortunately there are other similar churches in existence, from which we can glean more detail and, also, parts of the masonry still survive.

The first mention one can find of the church is around 1251, when Sir Thomas de Ednesoure gave 'to the nuns of Polesworth a piece of ground within his lordship of Badsley Ednesoure containing 125 foot in length and 61 in breadth'. This land was confirmed to them in 1297, by Richard de Herthull, when Sir Richard 'gave to the nuns of Polesworth, and to the Chapell of St Nicholas at Badsley [of which manor he was lord] that messuage and a half-yard land, which those nuns had held of his ancestors in Badsley aforesaid. and on Will. Silvester, vicar there, and his successors there, he bestowed a certain tenement, which Alan the precedent vicar held in the time of his ancestor Will Sauvage.'

Two things spring to mind from all this: in the time of the Sauvages, around 1166, there was a vicar in Baddesley, named Alan; and there was a chapel in Baddesley at that time.

Although Baddesley enjoyed the services of a vicar in the twelfth century, he was under the domination of the nuns of Polesworth and, no doubt, Baddesley was within their leet. After the Dissolution, however, the vicar of Polesworth was also the vicar of Baddesley.

Prior to the Dissolution the whole of the church in Britain was Roman Catholic. Because of the Catholic belief in Purgatory (where the souls of the dead were held, while it was decided whether they should go to heaven or to hell) people left land and money to the church and other religious institutions, such as monasteries, hoping that it would influence the decision which way the soul went.

Over the years monasteries had gained so much land in this way that they had become more like land management companies. For instance, the monastery at Merevale enclosed the village of Bentley in the fifteenth century simply driving the villagers out, as it was more profitable to run sheep on the land than have the villagers living there. The only signs of the old village left is one end of the church wall standing in a field and the path of the village streets in the field which can still be discerned.

Church House, built around 1850 with masonry from the old church.

Moreover, as the English monasteries were often satellites of parent monasteries in France, a tremendous amount of money was being sent to France. At the time England was the only European country without a standing army as the King had not the money to sustain one.

King Henry VII took steps to prevent the outflow of money. But Henry VIII went further, for a number of reasons. He was covetous of the huge land holdings of the monasteries; he had espoused the anti-papist teachings of Martin Luther; and he wanted a divorce from his brother Arthur's widow, Catherine of Aragon, to whom he had been married as a boy. He wanted sons, and she had only been able to provide him with one sickly son. He was also enamoured of Anne Boleyn. The only person able to grant him a divorce was the Pope, but the Pope of the day was virtually a prisoner of the King of Spain, Catherine of Aragon's brother.

As a way out of all his problems, Henry took the step of creating the Church of England, with himself as its head, abolishing Catholicism. All the clergy had to swear allegiance to Henry as head of the church, to retain their livings.

It is possible that the vicar of Baddesley at this time was a 'recusant', one of those who chose not to recognise Henry. After the Dissolution Baddesley had lost its vicar, so the vicar of Polesworth was also vicar of Baddesley. This situation remained until the middle of the seventeenth century.

It is not clear who was the first perpetual curate of the village but mention has been found of Peter Mousall, minister in 1671, with John Hunter as churchwarden. But the earliest parish register was for 1688, the first priest signing himself as 'Curate', so from at least that time Baddesley regarded itself as being a seperate entity.

In 1799 the vicar of Polesworth mentioned a composition, approved by the Bishop, by which Baddesley became an independent parish in 1687. The residents of Baddesley could select a curate, but the vicar of Polesworth was to approve. The curate could have all tythes, mortuaries and oblations for which rates were paid, but the vicar of Polesworth was to be paid eight shillings [40p] a year by the Baddesley church-wardens. A footnote stated that the Baddesley Lords of the Manor had chosen a curate without seeking his approval, and he had never been paid any eight shillings in his term as vicar.

He went on to say that he found, in his predecessor's book of dues, some 27 inhabitants of Baddesley who owed dues to the vicar of Polesworth, amounting to 6s 9d [64p]. ' Mem: I employed John Clifford the clerk of Baddesley , ye last sa.... to collect ye dues, and he brought me two shillings and seven pence. Half a crown he had for his trouble and a penny I received. I have crossed those names that paid and there has been an alteration of ye inhabitants since Mr Cotterill's [his predecessor] collection, I have made them to my list.'

The vicars of Polesworth seem to have kept trying to collect their dues from the Baddesley people, but did not seem to have got very far.

The New Church

By the 1840s the churchwardens and vicar had problems. The old Norman church was no longer large enough for the growing community, it was beginning to get run down, and also the mining activities on the Low Common had left the church isolated from the site where the village was growing. Whereas their rivals, the Congregational church and the newly formed Wesleyan Methodists, were more conveniently placed.

So, while other parish churches were being enlarged (for instance St Mary's at Atherstone) at Baddesley they opted for a new church and petitioned Bishop John of Lichfield for permission to build one.

The churchwardens, George Harris and William Crossley, and the curate, the Rev William Bradley MA (who had been appointed perpetual curate in

St Nicholas church, erected 1846.

1818), were the authors of the petition, claiming that the church was 'very ancient and dilapidated and pronounced unsafe for divine worship, and would hold not more than 265 persons'. The dilapidation was due in no small measure to the activities of the curate himself who had deliberately dilapidated the church to further his claims. Bishop John granted a faculty for a new church in 1845, providing that sufficient of the old church be left 'for reading the burial service' and the old churchyard to continue to be used. (Despite this, as soon as the new church was built, the old one was ruthlessly demolished and parts sold.)

The plans for building the new church started. Mr Dugdale, as the major Lord of the Manor, gave a plot of land for the purpose. The largest part of the money for the project, some £3,600, was raised by the local community in the form of donations and a church rate. The Society for Promoting Church Accomodation donated £100 and the Incorporating Society gave £75.

Mr Dugdale had just completed the building of his new hall at Merevale. The architect responsible for the completion of the hall, Mr Henry Clutton, was commissioned to design and build the new church. However Pevsner's *Warwickshire* (in his series 'The Buildings of England'), written in conjunction with Alexandra Wedgwood, describes the church as the work of more than one man. One of the more unusual features of the church is the pulpit which is corbelled out from the wall, with its access by way of the vestry and the tower stairs.

Apart from the church records very little was brought from the old church to the new one. The only two exceptions are the smaller of the two bells, the one and a half hundredweight [75kg] bell cast for the old church in 1706, by Joseph Smith of Edgbaston. The other was a small beaten silver chalice, thought to be the one purchased in the seventeeth century by the curate of the day.

The church clock, built by John Smith and Son of Derby, was installed on July 6th 1920 as part of the Village's War Memorial. However, it was the subject of some controversy and in 1933 the Parochial Church Council accepted trusteeship of it.

The second, larger bell is one weighing fourteen hundredweights, two quarters and eleven pounds [667kg], cast for the new church when it was built by C. and G. Mears of London.

One wonders what sort of musical accompaniment was used in the early days of the new church's life, as it was not until 1889 that an organ was fitted and that one was a barrel organ. It was built and installed by J. Parritt of Leicester. The finger organ, also by J.Parritt, was bought in 1900 at a cost of £210. Money was raised by subscriptions, a bazaar, working parties and collections. The organ was opened by the Rt Rev Dr Knox, Bishop of Coventry when there was a large congregation. Parritts were paid off on July 12th 1900.

As a matter of interest, there are a number of photographs of the interior of the church taken before the electric lights were installed, showing the wrought iron standards bearing the old oil lamps, which were attached to the ends of the pews up the aisle. These photographs can be dated in that, on some of them, the left hand or northern shaft of the chancel arch is visible. These were taken before the finger organ was installed, as this stands out further than the old barrel organ used to, and obscures the view of the chancel arch shaft.

Demolition of the old church

Despite the bishop's ruling that sufficient of the old church be retained for the reading of the Burial Service, as soon as the new church was completed the old one was ruthlessly demolished and the parts sold off. St Mary's church at Atherstone was being renovated and enlarged at the time. Abraham Bracebridge resided in Atherstone Hall, immediately behind St Mary's, was a millionaire banker whose family had made millions out of the misfortune of others when the South Sea Bubble burst. He bought the old church's doorway and had it inserted in the rear of St Mary's as a private entrance for himself and his family. It is still there, a good specimen of a decorated small Norman church doorway.

Attleborough were building their church, so they bought the triangular font. It was used for a few years before the vicar decided to buy a new one. So the old Baddesley font was turfed out into the churchyard where it may still be seen, mouldering away.

The pulpit was known to everyone as Latimer's Pulpit after Bishop Latimer who was burned at the stake in Oxford in 1555, together with Bishop Cranmer, by Queen Mary because he was one of those responsible for giving Mary's father, Henry VIII, tuition in the teachings of Martin Luther. When Mary came to the throne Latimer tried to keep out of sight by visiting his relatives, the Glover family, at Baxterley Hall. This was adjacent to Baxterley church and the site is commemorated by cottages named Latimers Rest. This is less than a mile from the old Baddesley church and, knowing of Latimer's love of preaching, it is quite reasonable to accept the old tradition that he preached from the old church's pulpit. At the time of the demolition the Wesleyan Methodists had recently leased the old Quaker Meeting House for use as a chapel. They bought the five-sided pulpit with its large sounding board. After a few adventures it is today standing in the Methodist Chapel.

The masonry was transported up to the village and used in building Church House. This was intended as a public house but was never used as such, being instead a shop with an outdoor beer license. When the masonry was being moved there was a tradition in the village that little men came during the night and took some of it back. This tale is common whenever old church masonry was re-employed but in Baddesley the story was given a new twist. The little

34

men were referred to as 'Twetter men' as, when they passed, they would say to each other, 'I twet, do you twet?'

One of the window arches was set over an entry in a row of cottages adjoining Church House, known as Church Row - but in the village it was 'the Gullet'. This is interesting as 'gullet' is a derivation of an Anglo-Saxon word meaning 'gallows tree'. One wonders whether there was a gallows tree somewhere in the vicinity. When the Gullet was demolished the Norman window arch was erected on the ground in front of the church tower.

Devious deals by the Living

White's Gazetteer for 1850 tells us that the living was a perpetual curacy, value £106, augmented with £1,200 Queen Anne's Bounty and £200 parliamentary grant, in the patronage of the parishioners. The population was 579, having risen from 371 in 1801, 335 in 1821 and 568 in 1831.

When Mrs Sarah Ball, the licensed victualler at the Red Lion Inn, died on April 23rd 1880 she left a bequest for the poor and sick of the parish. The church and churchwardens took over the trusteeship of the bequest. Claiming that the living was only £70 per year, with a population of 932, they took £1,014 from the bequest to augment the living, leaving a matter of £300 for the poor and sick. After the Parish Council had been formed the Councillors undertook the trusteeship of the bequest, and provided surgical appliances for the use of the sick, from the interest on the capital. But inflation overtook the bequest and it was amalgamated with the much better-financed Merevale Aid in Sickness charity whose function was very similar.

The New Churchyard

There is no record to hand when the new churchyard was opened, but the old one continued to be used after the old church's demolition, as there are gravestones there dating up to the early 1860s. It can only be presumed that the old churchyard closed and the new one opened around that time. The new graveyard surrounded the new church and was raised up, supported by a dry stone wall. This in turn being surrounded by a ditch, probably in deference to the shallow water table. Around the perimeter alternate lime trees and yew trees were planted, but cattle in adjacent fields ate foliage from the yew trees with tragic results, whereupon the yew trees were removed from the perimeter, leaving only the lime trees. The graveyard extension was consecrated at a ceremony held in January 1927.

The upkeep of the churchyard was paid for by parishioners, on a voluntary basis. A few of the church's faithfull's would collect 1d a month. An old neighbour and friend of mine, Mrs Charlotte Smith (wife of 'Tom' Smith), was out most Friday evenings collecting pennies, sometimes for the churchyard and other times for the Merevale Nursing Association - from the assets of which the Merevale Aid in Sickness charity was set up.

Around 1960 it was argued that only a few parishioners contributed a penny a month, whereas all the village claimed the right to the use of the churchyard. So it was put to the Parish Council that they should undertake employing a parishioner on a part-time basis to tend the churchyard, paid for out of the parish rate. The Parish Council adopted the idea and, after consulting the parishioners at an annual Parish Meeting, it was put into practice. A churchyard committee was set up and the Parish Council paid £156 per year (£3 per week) into the committee's funds, and still does so.

In the church is a memorial to the tragic occurrence at the nearby Stratford Pits on May 2nd 1882, when 37 rescuers were trapped underground by an explosion, while trying to rescue nine men entombed by an underground fire. A plaque bears the names of the three men and a boy, members of the entombed workers who died, and four of the rescuers who also perished (all parishioners) and of the mine owner who succumbed from his injuries.

The Old Vicarage

The vicarage seems to have been moved twice, first from its old site in the 'Old Zach's' - probably the parcel of land presented to Alan by Sir Thomas de Ednesore - which gained the name 'Old Zach's' from Zachariah Wragge, who was vicar of both Polesworth and Baddesley. It then moved to the grounds of the present vicarage, on a parcel of the common, one of the highest points in the village. A 1780 map of the village shows a schoolroom at Higg's Corner, an 'Old Vicarage' on Post Office Road, opposite the old Post Office, which later became the Vicarage orchard. This map shows a 'New Vicarage' on the other side of the Vicarage grounds on the site to the old vicarage (which has become the site of the newer, existing one). No other mention has ever been found of the 'Old Vicarage' other than this reference on the old map; it indicates that today's vicarage is the third to have been built in the vicarage grounds.

The last vicarage would appear to have been built in the middle of the eighteenth century, then added to and the grounds enlarged in the middle of the nineteenth century - but the windows frames of the older portion were used in

The last Vicarage, demolished in the 1950s.

the enlarged version. However, there are no records of either the original building or of the enlargement. It was a fine old house, with coach houses and stables, lawns and tennis courts, and a large orchard, the whole surrounded with beech trees. By around 1960 it had detoriorated and, in any case, was now considered too large. It was demolished and replaced by the more-modern present-day vicarage.

Between the two World Wars, from 1919 to 1939, the vicarage and its outbuildings - the old stables and coach houses - housed a number of village organisations. The Mothers' Union, Wolf Cub Pack, Girl Guides and Brownies met in a room in the vicarage itself. The Athletic Club, Boys Club, Senior Scouts and Rovers met in the outbuildings - a full-sized boxing ring being housed in the coach-house. There was a half-sized billiard table in the room above the coach house, together with a library, making it a focal point for the youths and young men of the village.

The activities these groups generated were many and varied, such as boxing matches on the Church Farm fields or the top floor of the Liberal Club and a twelve-mile cross-country race every Boxing day. The 1st Baddesley, St Nicholas Boy Scout Group paraded to church on the first Sunday each month, with their drum and bugle band.

The Sunday Schools, senior and junior, and the Bible Classes met in either the Infants School or the 'Stute. The 'Stute, sited in a corner of the vicarage orchard on Post Office Road (opposite the entrance to Hunters Park), was a large corrugated zinc sheet building which, originally, was the Church Hall. But from the 1929 to the 1950s it was the headquarters of the Boy Scout Group and afterwards the Army Cadets. The 'Stute' was demolished in the 1950s, and its site, together with the much of the orchard, sold as building plots. The bungalows in Post Office Road now stand there.

Notable clergy

One of the more memorable of the vicars was the Rev Wilson Lee, 'Parson Lee'. He was the parish vicar for a number of years until his death in 1921 and the tales of his activities used to be legion. One which comes to mind concerns the women of Baddesley who, before bus services started, customarily walked to Atherstone on shopping and market days. One of the most popular routes was by way of the footpath alongside the Middle School, through Grendon Wood, to the Watling Street. The footpath at the entrance to Grendon Wood became a morass of mud, to the distress of the women. Baddesley Parish Council could not do anything about it because it was outside their parish. Grendon Parish Council would not do anything about it as it did not affect many Grendon parishioners. Parson Lee personally bought cart loads of 'byard' (the pink shale from the burned out pit dirt mounds) and resurfaced the footpath with his own two hands, to shame the two Parish Councils. Another time he had a stand up fight on the common with a parishioner who, it was alleged, ill-treated his wife and children.

The Rev H.E. Brighton, who in the 1930s joined whole-heartedly in all and every aspect of village life, was treated most unfairly by a national journal named *John Bull*. Mr Brighton was continually asking for assistance on behalf of one or another of the organisations in the village. In appealing on behalf of one such organisation, in the church magazine, he signed the article as 'Your begging vicar'. This was seized on and he received an undeserved public dressing down, especially in a national journal.

The Society of Friends in Baddesley

George Fox, the son of a weaver and founder of the Quaker movement, was born at Drayton on the Clay, now known as Fenny

Drayton, only a few miles from Baddesley. He had difficulty in reconciling himself with the teachings of the church of the day and travelled around the district seeking fellow spirits. At Baddesley he found one in the person of Anthony Brickley. Through Brickley he formed a small group of like-minded people from round about, meeting at Baddesley around 1645, 'to form the second Friends Meeting ever to be established', according to a well-known Quaker historian, Joe Pickrance, 'about seven years before George set eyes on Swarthmore Hall in 1652'. Swarthmore Hall, the home of Judge Fell, is generally accepted as the birthplace of the Quaker movement.

Fox's journal reads, 'The Truth first sprang to us, as to be a people of the Lord, in Leicestershire in 1644, and in Warwickshire (Baddesley) in 1645.' He goes on to describe travelling northward, eventually reaching Westmoreland and Swarthmore Hall in 1652.

Apart from two imprisonments, a short one at Nottingham and another of a year (when a John Fretwell and he were imprisoned in Derby), Fox spent several years around 1644-46 'travelling backwards and forwards in the counties of Leicester, Darby and Warwick'. He spent 1653 in Westmoreland and Lancashire gathering round him about 70 travelling ministers, then a preaching movement began southwards. He travelled slowly and passed through Leicestershire without visiting his family at Fenny Drayton, came to Baddesley where, he says, 'I came to Anthony Brickley's where there was a great meeting; at which several others came and jangled, but the Lord's power came over them'.

There can be little doubt that many of those who attended this and subsequent meetings became founders of meetings in North Warwickshire, as a reference to the early records shows that various assemblies were established just about that time. It is clear twenty Meetings had been gathered in as many miles in 1656.

It should be explained that the name Quaker was, and still is, a nickname for a member of the Society of Friends. Their religious services are known as Meetings, their congregations are also known as Meetings and their places of worship known as Meeting Houses. Fox's name for churches was 'Steeple Houses'.

There is a record in the Quarterly Meeting Book, a small scrap of paper, which reads: 'Margery Fretwell, which is Anthony Brickley's daughter gave an account that Richard Farnsworth of Tickhill in Yorkshire visited Badgely Ensor in the yeare of 1654; and he was entertained for severall weeks theare and he visited severall other places while he was theare'.

Manor Cottages, bought in 1659 by Nathaniel Pewter together with a croft at the top of Key's Mill, and presented to George Fox. The cottage became the Meeting House and the croft used as a Quaker graveyard.

The Manor Cottages as a Quaker Meeting House

Sited at the junction of Speedwell Lane and New Street, the Manor Cottages are a sandstone and rubble-built fifteenth century cottage, with a large mullioned window, to which a wing, consisting of two brick and timber built cottages, have been added. In 1669 Nathaniel Newton, who owned farms at Baxterley and Hartshill, bought the manor cottages, and a croft at the top of Key's Hill, and presented them to George Fox to use - the cottages as a Meeting House and the croft as a graveyard. The graveyard was neccesary as Quakers were excommunicated and barred from internment in churchyards. There are in the records of many local parishes mention of Quakers being sent to Baddesley for burial, as Baddesley Quaker burial ground was the only one in the district. One such, an entry in Polesworth church records, states: 'August 9th, 1670. William Harris, a Quaker excommunicated buried at Baddesley.'

The meetings at that time were estimated to be between 200 and 250 strong, with members of all ages. They came from towns and villages several miles from Baddesley. Between 1682 and 1687, 85 of them were presented at Quarter Sessions, for attending illegal meetings, or for failing to attend church for holy service.

40

The Quaker Meeting House, Baddesley, built in 1722.

From a scarcely-legible record we find that: 'Anthony Brickley [with whom both George Fox and Richard Farnsworth lodged] was, together with twenty-one other Baddesley Friends, imprisoned at Warwick for twenty six weeks for meeting together to worship God.' This was the first time that Quakers were mentioned in Warwickshire courts. During their imprisonment they were several times tempted to take the oath of allegiance, but refused to do so. They were visited during their captivity by George Fox.

During the Commonwealth, that is, while the country was being run by the Parliament without a monarch (the king having been beheaded), the Friends were often in conflict with the State. After the Act of Uniformity in 1662 the intensity of the persecution increased enormously. Persecution began in Baddesley in 1656. 'A poor widow, a member of the Baddesley meeting, was arbitrarily thrust out of her house by her landlord, Walter Chetwynd, and her goods on to the street; and when she reminded him that she could live there as long as she pleased, a promise made by his father, he replied "You were not a Quaker when he made that promise". Although she had had the land ploughed, he forbad her sowing it, saying "if she sows it I shall reap it".' Many other similar instances are recorded. As time went on the charges became more severe. When both husband and wife were charged with missing church on one Sunday only, the accused were confined to gaol till the next sessions.

41

Despite the persecution and 'meane persons' breaking up meetings, at its heyday the Meeting was the strongest in Warwickshire and remained strong until the 1750s.

In 1722, when religious bodies other than the Church of England were allowed to have meetings, the Baddesley Quakers built their own purpose-built Meeting House on the croft at the top of Key's Hill (which had been provided as a burial ground) together with a keeper's cottage and roomy stables for those who had to travel from afar to the meetings. The Meeting House stands today and is used as the Methodist's Sunday Schoolroom. The stables, alas, have gone and the keeper's cottage reduced to a single storey.

When the Meeting was moved from the Manor Cottages to the new Meeting House, the old buildings reverted to their original use as dwellings, and continued to be used as such until shortly before they were demolished in the mid-1950s. The old building stood way out so the street at that point was quite narrow. For the last fifty years of their existence, the sandstone portion was occupied by the Smallwood family, Benny Smallwood being one of the old village characters and many of his descendants live locally. Until they were demolished the cottages were visited annually by groups of Quakers, and since then the Keys Hill Meeting house has been visited regularly, and a meeting held. In 1992 a group of Quakers from Canada, U.S.A., Africa, New Zealand and Australia spent a couple of hours there.

The Quaker burial ground was marked as such on all of the mining maps, marked 'coal not to be got'. The Methodist church has, for financial reasons, had to sell the graveyard It was bought by the Borough Council and earmarked for the erection of single-person dwellings, but government policy has so far prevented this happening. Before the ground could be sold for building purposes it had to be proved that no one had been buried there for at least a hundred years.

At the time that Fox first visited Baddesley it was sparsely populated with almost everyone engaged in agricultural pursuits. Among them were several substantial yeomen, owning and cultivating their own freeholds. As in other parts of the country, it was from this class that the Society of Friends drew some its first and best members. Nathaniel Newton and Anthony Brickley were two such. Others were the Sharrat family, who owned and operated the Baddesley windmill. The last Baddesley windmill has been described as a simple post mill, with an open base. It was sited on the open space, still known as the Mill Knob (adjacent to the siren), and was dilapidated in the Corn Riots of 1756. Seaby's book *Warwickshire Windmills* records it 'was sailless by 1760'.

*The windmill which used to be sited on a high point of
Baddesley Common, known as Mill Knob.*

Quakers and the Corn Riots of 1756

Corn riots occurred between 1740 and 1845 as a result of the Corn
Bounty regulations of 1684. This was intended to be a way of subsidising
landowners by maintaining the price of agricultural produce. The government
paid a subsidy to anyone exporting agricultural produce with the result that
farmers could get a better price from exporting than they could on the home
market. When there was a surplus of produce, this worked fine. But when there
was a poor harvest the farmers continued selling to exporters to the
disadvantage of the rest of the population, creating hardship and actual
starvation for the poor. In the meantime, the farmers were enjoying the benefits
of the higher prices created by the Corn Bounty.

43

1756 was a particularly bad year for the farmers. Heavy and continuous rains caused the harvest to be late. This in turn caused a knock-on effect for the pits. The period of the year for the greatest coal sales was in the autumn, when coal was being bought for use in the winter. Traditionally, most of the carting of coal was done by the farmers after they had gathered in their harvest. Late harvest gathering led to mounting stocks of pit-head coal, causing miners to be laid off, so that miners had smaller wage packets at a time when the price of corn was rocketing. It shot up to between 67 and 72 shillings a quarter [£3.35 - £3.60 per 250kg] in May (from 22 to 26 shillings [£1.10 - £1.30] at the beginning of the year) - a price well outside the pocket of any working man. As usual the working people looked for someone to blame for this state of affairs, and as most of the Corn Factors were Quakers, the Quakers were blamed.

According to W.C. Braithewaite's *The Second Period of Quakerism* the miners of Baddesley and Ansley were the first to riot that year, attacking and irreparably damaging the Quaker-owned windmill at Baddesley, then attacking the Quaker Meeting Houses at Atherstone and Hartshill. The miners of Nuneaton, Bedworth and Coventry, spurred on and encouraged by their local communities, joined in and for a time they took and held the city of Coventry. Urging that grain should be sold in smaller quantities even though it was sent to market in bulk, they threatened that if the farmers did not sell their grain this way, they would sell it for them. Most miners in the region rioted, the one notable exception being the miners from the Polesworth and Wilnecote area.

Troops were brought in from Warwick and Northampton, a number of arrests made, and the miners dispersed. Sixteen were arrested on Friday, convicted on Saturday and hung, drawn and quartered on the Monday. Only one of these was from the Baddesley and Ansley area, a man named Charles Simpson. Four others were from Nuneaton.

Although it had remained strong up to that time, the Baddesley Quaker Meeting never recovered from these events and gradually faded away. In 1830 the Meeting House became disused and was taken over by the Wesleyans in 1836.

Nonconformist Churches

There are two Nonconformist churches in the village, the Wesleyan Methodists, and the United Reform Church, known in the past the Congregational Church. Just over the parish boundary, in Grendon, is a third, the Free Methodists. The two in the village are both on Key's Hill with the

Methodists at the top and the United Reform half-way down. So, they have always been known the parishioners as the 'Top Chapel' and the 'Bottom Chapel'. Even today the villagers refer to them as such, rather than by their proper titles. This is partly because the Top Chapel used to be known as the Wesleyan, and is now the Methodists, and Bottom chapel was always known as the Congregational, or 'Congs', and is now the United Reform.

Pre-war there were very few residents did not belong to one of the chapels or to the church. Thanks to their membership of the Sunday School Union, the elders of the chapels met and worked with each other. For instance, choirs of all three chapels joined forces at each other's Sunday School Anniversaries, or 'Sermons', and at Harvest Fetivals etc. The Church of England stood apart, and at times was openly hostile to the chapels. Only a few years ago, the parish vicar, Canon Williams, referred to chapel members as 'heathens'.

The teenage members of the chapels were catered for by organisations such as the Methodist Guild. The teenagers met weekly playing table tennis, had guest speakers and, of course sang hymns, mostly from the old Sankey Hymn Books. Exchange visits with other Guilds took place. One of the favourites was with Dordon, the youngsters quite happily walking to and from each other's venues.

Both chapels ran football teams - these originated in the Bible Classes. Both teams were notorious as hard players, deservedly or not. The last of the chapel teams was the Congregational team, known as the 'Congs'. This team folded in the mid-1920s, to be replaced by the Baddesley Old Boys.

Both chapels played quite a part in the social life of the village, catering for christenings, weddings and burial services. Or hatching, batching and despatching.

The Bottom Chapel

The Bottom Chapel, or Congregational Chapel, owed its foundation to a Hartshill-born man, John Dagley, who set up the chapel at Chapel End in 1804, before turning his attention to Baddesley and later to Ansley. In 1820 he wrote a poem in which he drew a thumbnail sketch of Baddesley, at the time that he was trying to form a Congregational Church in the village. It appears that the local vicar, referred to in the poem as 'a reverend doctor', paid the Baddesley men with drink to break up the meetings that Dagley held. The poem goes:

'A most abandonded place it was
I wish to tell you the cause;
A colliery it was indeed
And in this way they did proceed:
After working hard all week
On Sabbath days they then would seek
Their cocks and dogs and make them fight
In this they did take great delight;
They drank, they swore and fought themselves
Their wives and children wretched too
I thought some good here I might do.'

Dagley seems to have been well-received in the village, perhaps too well, as the vicar of the day took steps to dissuade him.

'A reverend doctor they had got,
Who lived on the very spot;
Became enraged, he thought it wrong
For a man, like me, to use my tongue
Therefore with men he did conbine
To give them ale, that's very fine,
To meet with me the next Lord's day
And from the place take me away.'

However, Dagley had managed to gain the support of two burly miners who, it seems, acted as bodyguards for him.

'But we had the strength of all,
For Bown and Jones were strong and tall
They fixed themselves each by my side
And their fists they often tried
Expecting to have to use them
In knocking down these drunken men.'

It goes on to say that the drunkards thought better of it and left him alone.

After this, Dagley formed a Congregational church in the village. Their meetings were held in a cottage in Hunters Piece, now Hunters Park.

The cottage had a balcony inserted in place of an upstairs floor, to increase its capacity. It ceased being used as a chapel when the existing chapel was built in 1864 and then reverted to use as a cottage. The older members of the community will remember it as the dwelling of one of the old Baddesley characters, Mr 'Jotto' Dingley.

The present chapel was also extended by having a balcony inserted. It also had its own burial plot at the rear, but this became full in the 1920s and no interments have taken place in it since. The usual practice is for a Burial Service to be held in the chapel, followed by an interment in St Nicholas' graveyard or by cremation at one or other of the cematoriums. The same proceedure is followed at the Methodist chapel.

The Top Chapel

The Quaker movement in the village survived and even thrived through the traumas of the seventeenth century Commonwealth period, when they were penalised and persecuted for their faith. They rapidly lost their local support after the Corn Riots, particularly the one of 1756, when the miners blamed the Quakers for the high prices of grain. By 1836 the movement had faded away completely in this area, and the newly-formed Wesleyan movement took a lease on the Meeting House for use as their Sunday schoolroom and later as a chapel.

The old St Nicholas church was demolished a few years later and parts sold off. The Wesleyans bought its black oak pulpit, several centuries old, to install in their chapel. This had been dubbed 'The Latimer Pulpit', by the local legend that during the reign of 'Bloody Queen Mary' the Bishop Latimer had preached from it shortly before his arrest, trial and burning at the stake.

Around the turn of the century the Methodists bought the Meeting House, and its other buildings, together with the burial plot which surrounded it, from the Quakers. They then built the existing chapel, connected to the old Meeting House with an inter-connecting door. To put in the connecting door they had to cut away part of the Quaker Elders' Bench, an integral part of the Meeting House, so that only the two ends of the bench are left. The purchase included the cottage known as the Governess' Cottage, which stood at the end of the Meeting House. To make the purchase and to build the new chapel they had to borrow money from their congregation and other parishioners. The village butcher, Mr Albert Walker, loaned them £100 and, as with other organisations - what with older members passing on and newer ones taking over - this debt was overlooked. When it was realised, the money was paid back. But only a few months later Mr Walker died of a heart attack in his air raid shelter, during an air raid, on May 5th 1941.

The congregation at both Top and Bottom chapels has dwindled over the years, until now there are talks being held to consider a merger.

The Baddesley and Grendon Sunday School Union

It was in 1891 that the idea of a Sunday School Union was first mooted. Seemingly, the Congregational Sunday School first suggested it and, at a meeting held on June 6th of that year, it was suggested that a Union be formed

The cottages around the White Horse Inn, known as The End, c.1930.. One of the old street taps is in the foreground.

and that the other Sunday Schools be approached. The Baddesley Wesleyans and the Grendon Free Methodists expressed their interest, but the St Nicholas Church of England Sunday School had no wish to particpate.

Accordingly a Union was formed temporarily, and a procession round the village was arranged to take place on Tuesday August 5th 1891. This must have been considered a success as, on August 12th, the joint committee met again and decided to make the Union a permanent one, and ensure that the schools worked together as harmoniously as possible.

Acting on this resolution, the joint committee got to work and organised the first Sunday School tea, for all the pupils of the three Sunday Schools, which was held on the November 3rd 1891 in the Wesleyan Chapel, Baddesley.

On August 5th 1892 a resolution was passed that a Code of Rules be drawn up for the proper working of the Union. This was done and the rules were read and unanimously approved on September 15th 1892. Each year after that a procession took place on the Tuesday following the August Bank Holiday Monday.

In 1899 it was decided that a joint open air service should be held on the common. This was held for the first time on July 30th of that year. All three of the churches represented in the Union met together for prayer and praise with short addresses on Sunday School work. The service was deemed to be a success and the practice has continued up to the present time. In 1992 the Daw Mill Colliery Band provided the accompaniment and it was estimated that over a thousand people were present. Thanks to the new vicar, Rev Keith Hodson, members of the Church of England church were encouraged for the first time to attend the Day of Praise.

The procession was always known as 'The Band Going Up The End', 'The End' being the Newlands Road of today. On nineteenth century maps of both mining and property Newlands Road is shown as 'The End'. And any Baddesley pensioner, if asked about 'The Band Going Up The End', automatically thinks of the August Tuesday Sunday School procession.

Bank Holidays

Until 1937 the miners had just two days holiday at August, the statutory Bank Holiday and the following day. On the Monday, there was the Atherstone Flower Show, held in Merevale Park. This was quite a prestigous affair, probably comparable with the county shows of today, with a military band, trick riding dispay, tent-pegging by a troop of cavalry, side shows and the like, in addition to the customary flower and produce exhibitions by both local gardeners and seed companies. The day always finished with a firework display, and a good view of this could be had from Folly Lane. So, those of the parishioners who could not afford to visit the Flower Show had a taste of it after dark by watching the firework display from the Folly.

But August Tuesday, that was Baddesley's day, the band went up the End. Pupils of the three Nonconformist Sunday Schools met at the Grendon chapel. Lead by a band they would parade out on to Watling Street, to the end of Spon Lane, turn about to the Black Swan, then back to the Boot Inn, and on up Boot Hill. Stopping at each turn, and joined by onlookers, they would sing one of the old Sankey Hymns.

St Nicholas' Sunday School, with a band of their own, would wait at the top of the hill and either precede or follow the others round the village. The parade dispersed near the Infants' School, the children making their way to their own Sunday School venues where a tea was provided for them. In the evening two fields had been arranged (one for the church the other for the chapels) where, to the accompaniment of music provided by their bands, there were races and games for the children with dancing for the adults.

The parade around the village coincided with the men turning out of the pubs and the Club and, of course, they joined in - in good voice, one might add.

From the late 1920s until the war, one of the popular week-end pastimes was 'mystery trips' run by the local bus companies, usually 'Evans', or 'Alec's' (as the De Luxe Coaches were known). These took place typically on Sunday evenings. One or two coach loads of parishioners would be taken for a ride around the countryside, stopping at some pub or club for a drink. When a party of people got togther, either on a bus or in a pub, whether they were accompanied by a piano or not, they would sing. Having sung their way through their repertoire of songs of the day, and of yesteryear, what was more natural than to sing the old Sankey Hymns that everyone knew and had been singing all their lives? The locals, wherever the bus load happened to have stopped at, would look askance, probably thinking that Baddesley was some sort of religious enclave.

Chapter 3
Village Schools

The Old Ivy House

Lower House or, as it was more widely known, 'The Old Ivy House', was a large two-storied, timber-framed building, some of the brick infilling being in herring bone pattern. As the name would suggest, it was covered in ivy. The front solar had collapsed, so that the whole of the front gaped open. It was commonly believed to be haunted and most people passing it at night had a feeling of dread. Several were adamant that they had seen the ghostly figure of a woman carrying a lighted candle inside it, walking either up or down a staircase. It stood opposite the junction of Watery Lane and Lower House Lane, and had to be demolished in the 1950s to enable Lower House Lane to be straightened at the time of upgrading to a 'B' road. All that remains of the Old Ivy House is a pile of rubble at the roadside.

The Old Ivy House was the residence of George Abbot when he died in 1647. Abbot was the son of Mrs Purefoy and stepson of Col William Purefoy of Caldecote Hall. Col Purefoy was one of the regicides, i.e. those who signed the death warrant of King Charles I. He was a Member of Parliament and actively engaged in the Civil War against the King.

George Abbot served two terms as a Member of Parliament for Tamworth, and it has been said that his father was Archbishop of Canterbury, although others refute this. He seems to have been a controversial figure. One school of thought regards him as a hero figure. During the Civil War, in the absence of his step-father, who was away serving in the Parliamentary army, George and his mother together with a few servants defended Caldecote Hall for several days, when it was besieged by a troop of Royalists.

Another school holds the opposite view, saying that he had his own 'private army', a band of ruffians; that he was actively engaged in

The Old Ivy House, George Abott's residence at the time of his death in 1647.

dispossessing ordinary people and enclosing common lands. A list of five or six villages in the Red Gate area exists, villages that it is alleged were enclosed by him, the names of which are now only the names of farms. It is said that he used his position as MP to steer Enclosure Acts through the house.

In his several pages-long will, Abbot left bequests to a number of men, at least two of whom were later presented at court for acts of violence. One of Abbot's lessees, Francis Lakyn, a violent character, was presented in court on a number of occasions. Once was for breaking into the close in Baddesley belonging to Sir Henry Willoughby, called Hunters Close (now called Hunters Park) and keeping possession. Other times were for 'grievously assaulting John Thompson' and for 'grievously assaulting one Thomas Levinge, gentleman'.

In his will George made numerous bequests, to be paid for out of his lands at Baddesley. His mother and his stepfather (whom he addressed as his father-in-law) held his estate and administered his bequests during their lifetime. After their deaths ownership passed to Daniel Barfield. Mr Barfield appears to have inherited the estate as he was living in Baddesley when his wife, Mary, died and was buried in Baddesley in April 1688. The inheritance did not seem to have worked for him very well, according to local legend, which has it that he could not pay his dues and so deliberately dilapidated the house and vacated it. The dues were presumably all Abbot's bequests which he had to pay annually.

To Baddesley residents, the most interesting of Abbot's bequests was 'I give and bequeath to commence after my Mothers death out of my lands at Badsley in Warwickshire the Sum of Foure Pounds and ten shillings per Annum forever for a Salary for a free school to teache Pettys both boys and girls of that Town and the Poor of any other Towns and parishes that shall send them, to read English perfectly and say by heart Mr. Ball's little Catechism'.

He also left a similar amount for a school at Caldecote. He went on 'Also out of the said Lands of Badsley forever I bequeath Twenty Shillings per Annum, Ten Shillings a piece to buy School books and Catechisms [for the schools at Caldecote and Baddesley].'

Five pounds a year was also left to augment the stipend of the vicar of Baddesley which had dwindled over the years to £4.10s [£4.50]. In Rev Bradley's time, 1886, he was receiving £4.10s a year from land held by a Capt Hincks. 'Parson Lee' (Rev Wilson Lee), when he first came to the village, had to chase the money up. Morris and Shaw, owners of Birch Coppice Colliery, when they purchased Lower House Farm (now known as the Skin Farm) invested £360 in Consols, from which the vicar receives £4.10s a year and, until the Church of England School (the Infants' School) closed, received £4.10s a year paid into the School Managers' Funds.

Church of England or Infants' School

How the village's schooling benefited as a result of George Abbot's bequest is not clear. It has been assumed that the Baddesley vicars did the same as had happened at many other places, that is, the vicar held a school at the vicarage. The curriculum usually contained housework, cooking, laundering, sewing etc. for the girls and home handy man, gardening etc. for the boys - or any other work the vicar or his wife wished them to do. This would seem to be bourne out when we find that the Rev John Adamthwaite gave tuition to pupils in the vicarage in 1812. But a map of the village of around 1780 labels buildings standing on or near the site of The Stocks, New Street (Higg's Corner) as Colliers Cottages and Schoolroom, although no more is known of it.

Elsewhere is found 'From 1824 to 1833, there being no schoolmaster, no payments was made. It has been agreed, that the balance [of George Abbot's bequest] shall be paid, and employed, with other subscriptions, in the erection of a school. A small one was erected in 1840.'

The Church of England or Infants' School.

This was built on a parcel of the common, and became the Church of England School, or as it was widely known the 'Infants' School'. The Charity Commissioners had been set up by this time and one wonders whether the fact that they were looking at such bequests influenced the decision to build a school.

The school was built in three phases. The original building was the central two classrooms, with a sandstone bell tower on the western end, very similar in style to the Bentley old school. The two classrooms could be separated by a folding wooden partition. As the village grew, with more workers being attracted by the work provided by the bigger pits, it was necessary to enlarge the school. A third classroom was added at the eastern end in the 1870s. This was always known as the 'Governess' classroom'. Despite this extention and, around 1902, the further addition of another classroom at the western end - a room always used as the entrance class, or in village parlance 'the babbies' class' - the school still was not large enough to cope with all the children of the growing village. So, from eleven year's old, the pupils had to trudge up the Bentley Hill to Bentley School until they were 13 years old, this being the school-leaving age.

The New School

In 1912 a new school was built, just outside the parish boundary in Grendon, consisting of four brick-built classrooms and two wooden structures, each divided into four classrooms, with a central lobby and a separate brick-built handicraft classroom, the 'Woodwork Class'. There was a minor

54

hiccup before construction could be started. To enter the proposed school one had to cross a strip of the common, a matter of four or five yards wide, and the Parish Council, very conscious of encroachment of the common, held up the construction work until they received reassurances on the matter. This school, the Baddesley Ensor Central School, was (and still is to the older parishioners) known as the 'New School'. Today, it is the Middle School. The opening of this school ended the daily trudge up Bentley Hill, to 'Boss Neale's' Bentley School.

The 'New School' was enlarged to its present size in 1931-32. While re-construction was carried out the two wood-constructed buildings were re-erected in the field which is now the site of Oakwood Close. The seven-to-eleven year olds used these and the over-eleven's had once more to trudge up to Bentley School, this time under 'Boss Hooper'.

The first headmaster at the 'New School', Mr Robert Wrenn Foster ('Old Foster', as he was popularly known) left the post temporarily to serve in the Royal Navy during World War I. He returned on demobilisation and held the post until his death during World War II. Another of the headmasters, Mr Ron Handley, also served in the Royal Navy. He first came to the school in the mid-1930s and served in the Fleet in the Second World War. He moved to the Atherstone High School with the over-eleven year old children in 1957, was appointed headmaster at Baddesley a few years later, and remained there until his retirement.

By 1947 classrooms in the New School had become vacant, for lack of pupils, and the two oldest classes of the Infants' School were moved over the common to the New School, leaving only the two lower classes at the old school. At this time the county library was using the old Governess' classroom on each Tuesday and Friday. Then, in 1957, the over-eleven's were moved to the Atherstone High School, travelling there by bus each day, leaving several more classrooms empty at the New School. The last two infant classes were moved across the common to occupy them. The Infants' School was handed to the Church of England, who used it for six or seven years as a church hall. It was then demolished and the ground sold as building plots.

The First School

In the 1950s, in the days when it was beleived by everyone, including the Lords of the Manor, that the Parish Council held a Common Right, the Parish Council received a letter from the Lords of the Manor, requesting permission to sell the triangular piece of the common to the County Council, to build a school on. No information was obtainable regarding the type of school envisaged, so the Parish Council were in a cleft stick. They did not want to deprive the village of a school, neither did they want to see the common eroding away, creating a precedent for any further sales of parcels of the common. After agonising over the matter for some time they decided against.

Some time later it was learned that the County Council had bought a large block of land at the bottom of Boot Hill. On enquiring it was learned that it was for a school. But no amount of querying could find what kind of school was intended.

A couple of years later the County Educational Committee called for a joint meeting of the managers of Bentley, Grendon and Baddesley school managers and disclosed that the County proposed to build a First School to take all the infants from the three parish schools, and to close the Grendon and Bentley schools. It was further revealed that there were three times as many toddlers in Baddesley as in the other parishes put together, but the managers of both Grendon and Bentley schools argued that their village schools should be kept open and the Baddesley toddlers be sent to augment their numbers. As one Bentley manager said 'the Baddesley parents could pop their children into their cars and take them to Bentley'.

When it was pointed out to the Educational Committee representative that the proposed site was at the bottom of a one-in-four hill, he replied that the site was in Baddesley, and that there was no site nearer Baddesley that could be used. The meetings were being held in the then Central School and it was pointed out to him that there was an expanse of nearly eighty acres of derelict land, the old outcrop workings, immediately behind him.

The ladies of the village got wind of the proposals and, after a public meeting where the villagers met the Education Committee's representatives, the site now occupied by the First School was decided on with access by way of Maypole Lane. This placed the proposed school outside the parish in the same way that the Middle School is outside the parish. When the lady who then occupied the position of chairperson to Baddesley Parish Council met county officials on the site, she asked if sufficient land could be included for two swimming pools, at some time in the future. And this request was acceded to.

As for the land purchased as a site at the bottom of Boot Hill, part of it was made into a sports field for the residents of Grendon. Even though it is in Baddesley. The rest of it was used as a site for a Council bungalow estate for the elderly, Penmire Close.

56

Chapter 4

Local Industry

Prior to the advent of the canals and the railways, two ingredients were essential for any community to thrive. They had to have some sort of natural resources and a means of transporting the products. Although the Warwickshire coalfield was the coalfield nearest to London, at one time not a cobble of Warwickshire coal was sold there. The capital, the biggest market for coal in the country, was captured by the Durham mines, for the simple reason that the Durham coalfield were sited on navigable rivers. Down these coal was transported to a fleet of collier ships which could easily reach the heart of London, via the North Sea and the Thames.

Incidentally, coal transported to London by this means was known as 'sea coal' as opposed to coal sold from collieries inland, which sold their coal from a 'landsale'. Fortunes were lost trying to find means of getting coal to the cities from the coalfields. It is said that the price of coal doubled for every five miles it was transported overland. So, until the canal arrived, the coal from Baddesley was confined to supplying local demand.

By today's standards roads were a joke until macadamised roads were introduced. Roads were simply strips of land up to fifty yards wide, along which drivers chose the least churned up path. It is on record that passengers in coaches drowned when their coaches sank into a morass of mud. Each parish was responsible for the roads on their 'patch'. In the 1600s the residents of Baddesley were presented at court 'for the digging of coals on the road known as the Watling Street'. A glance at a map will show that the only bit of the Watling Street in Baddesley is the few hundred yards between the Boot Inn, and White's Farm where the Penmire Brook (which forms the parish boundary) crosses the Roman road. On another occasion, the Parish Highway Supervisor and Churchwardens were presented for 'neglecting their duties'.

In the late seventeenth century there were quite a few tramways in and around Baddesley prior to the canal reaching the district in the 1700s. The tramways were built to get coal to the Watling Street. In fact, most of the footpaths and lanes leading to the Watling started life as tramways. But the information on early tramways is very limited regarding the rail gauges, types of rails and wheels used, size of trams etc., making it most difficult to build up a picture of what was being done, when and why. It seems that the more information one collects the more questions one finds unanswered.

The only tramway that one could even guess at is the earliest one. This was on what was then Grendon common, land recently purchased from Sir George Chetwynd by Mr Stratford, who then leased the mining rights to Messrs England and Burslem. It is interesting to note that Burslem had earlier conducted a survey of all of Mr Straford's holding at Baddesley. In 1740 Messrs England and Burslem put in a tramway from their drift mines in Grendon Wood, to the Watling, following the line of the existing footpath, alongside the Black Ridding. The cuttings and embankments of this tramway may still be seen. This tramway almost certainly used wooden wheels and rails as iron ones had not been introduced at that time. However subsequent lease-holders, mining in the same area, using the same tramway route, used metal plates or rails and, of course, metal-wheeled trams.

Much later, at the beginning of this century, when the parishes had to put in their own sewages (around 1901 or 1902) the Grendon Parish Council put in an underground sewage pipe, down the Ridding, to serve the upper part of Grendon. They had this sewage pipe laid alongside the line of the old tramway, through the cutting. In excavating to lay the sewage pipe, the cutting was moved over a matter of three or four feet.

The last lease holder to work mines in this area was a Mr 'Tommy' Slack who was operating the Silver Birch drift mine there until three or four years before World War II.

The stumbling block for all early mine captains was the Watling Street. At the time of the greatest demand, in the winter, the Watling Street was at its muddiest. The coalowners petitioned Parliament several times for permission to turnpike the road, that is, for them to bear the cost of metalling the road then to be able to charge everyone else using the road a toll. In 1762 an Act was passed enabling them to not only turnpike the Watling Street, but also to turnpike adjoining roads. This done, the road transport position became easier.

One of the adjoining roads turnpiked was the Boot Hill and Coleshill Road. These were both re-aligned, Boot Hill being turned at the point which is now the bottom of St Nicholas Estate, across what was then Grendon

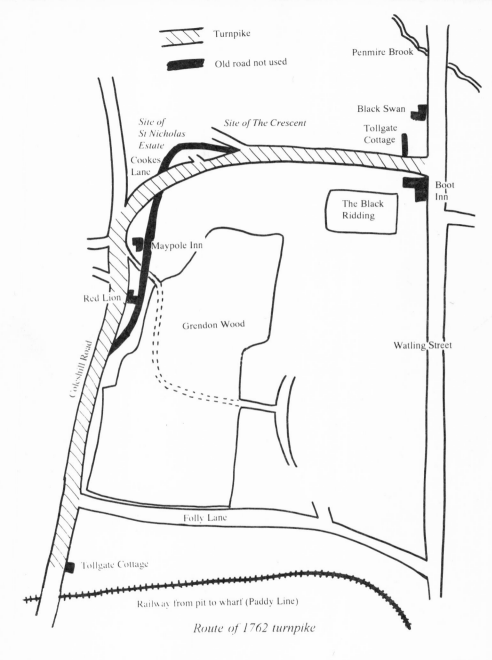

Turnpike

Old road not used

Penmire Brook

Black Swan

Site of
St Nicholas
Estate

Site of The Crescent

Tollgate
Cottage

Cookes
Lane

Boot
Inn

The Black
Ridding

Maypole Inn

Red Lion

Grendon Wood

Watling Street

Coleshill Road

Folly Lane

Tollgate Cottage

Railway from pit to wharf (Paddy Line)

Route of 1762 turnpike

59

The old Toll Gate Cottage on the Coleshill Road, near Baddesley Colliery.

Common. Prior to this Boot Hill had been straight from the Boot Inn to Cooke's Lane, the upper half travelling up the boundary of the St Nicholas Estate. The old Coleshill Road also was straight, along Cooke's Lane, across the Brickle Pits, behind the Maypole Inn, behind the Red Lion Inn, joining the existing Coleshill Road in front of the cottage always known to parishioners as 'Granny Ball's shop'.

The turnpike was taken out on to Baddesley Common up in front of the Red Lion Inn. The disused, top piece of Boot Hill diminished in importance until it became a footpath. This is still shown on the Ordnance Survey maps as a footpath and is the parish boundary, although for most of its length the residents of St Nicholas Estate have included its track in their gardens. The disused part of the old Coleshill Road is not recognised as a path of any description (that is, the stretch from the Brickle Pits, behind the new Maypole Inn and the Red Lion Inn).

The turnpike or Toll Road stretched from the rear of the Boot Inn, where one of the toll gate cottages used to stand, to the bottom of the hill between the Top Folly and the old Baddesley mine, where the other toll gate cottage stood. This was demolished only a few years ago, after the last resident passed away.

Coalmining

Coal mining is Baddesley's reason for being where it is. Mining activity killed off the village in its old site in the valley of the Penmire Brook, near the old churchyard. But where other villages withered and died, Baddesley got up and moved to its present site at the top of the hill (where, at the time, longer-lifed pits were being sunk, so there the employment was).

Thanks to the geological happenings approximately fifty million years ago, at the same time that the Penines were thrust up, the Warwickshire coalfield was presented with difficulties not encountered in other coalfields. A huge 'plug' was thrust up, together with its underground coal seams, reaching from Coventry in the south, to Nuneaton, curling round to Tamworth in the north. It was then subjected to tremendous side pressures, which squeezed it until it was concave, or saucer-shaped. Lying over the coal seams is an impervious layer of sandstone, which was also squeezed saucer-shaped, with the result that layers above the coal seams became waterlogged, not unlike a huge saucer, half-full of water. These water-bearing layers are correctly known as the 'Halesowen Beds'.

The coal was exposed on the surface (what is known as the 'basset' of the seams) all the way from Coventry to Tamworth, but descended rapidly, often as steeply as one in two-and-a-half, quickly descending below the water-bearing layers. The early pits excavated the coal on the surface, following the seams down until they disappeared under the wet layers, where they gave up and moved elsewhere.

When the Newcomen pumping engine was introduced, around 1730, quite a number were put to use in the Warwickshire coalfield, but they were very expensive to hire and operate, and caused a number of bankruptcies. There is no evidence of one being used at Baddesley, although Beaton's map of Warwickshire at that time might be construed as showing a 'fire engine', as they were known, in the Baddesley area.

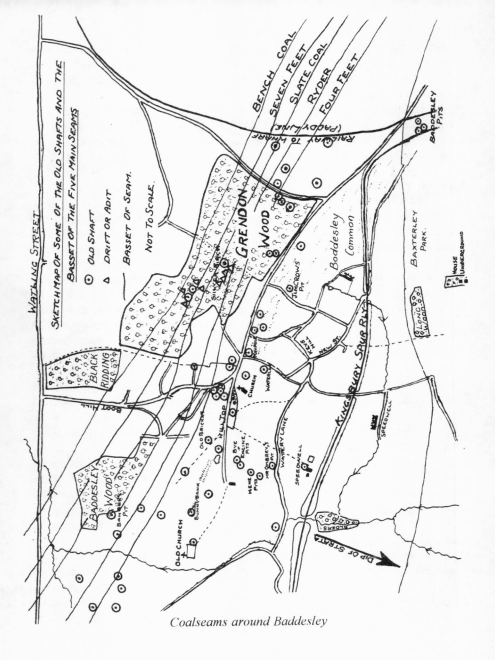

Coalseams around Baddesley

The coal seams are well separated in the north of the coalfield, as is shown on the sketch map, showing the bassets of the four main seams. But in the south of the field, the seams run together, forming a seam 24 feet thick. This thick seam is known as the 'Warwickshire Thick Seam', or as the 'Hawkesbury Thick Seam', as it was at Hawkesbury Colliery that it was first encountered. This is the seam worked at the Coventry Colliery, the newer Daw Mill Colliery, and several other collieries in the Coventry area. At Daw Mill sixteen feet of the seam is extracted. In the later days of the Baddesley Mine, as the workings reached further south, several seams ran together forming a sixteen feet thick band. At one period ten feet was being extracted.

The first recorded shaft at Baddesley was in the sixteenthth century, sunk by Sir Henry Willoughby. An old mining map shows a grid-iron pattern of shafts, only a few yards apart, on the common between Coleshill Road and Crow Hill and the Gullet, labelled 'ancient mines'. On a Ministry of Defence aerial photograph, taken in December 1948, one can discern a similar grid-iron pattern of shafts on the Folly side of Colliery Farm, Merevale. These were either 'Bell Pits', or pits working the Junker system.

The sketch map shows the basset of the four main seams, where they reached the surface. These ran roughly north-to-south and, of course, marked the edge or boundary of the coalfield. With the seams dipping sharply to the west, in the early days pitmasters had to contend with steeply inclined seams and wet conditions. More often than not the pits were closed by an inrush of water. The gradual improvement in newer, more efficient, pumping engines (first atmospheric, then steam followed by compressed air, then electrically-powered ones) has over the years made the water problem manageable.

When they got the coal to the surface there was the problem of getting it to the consumers. The advent of the macadamised turnpikes, then the canals (both being fed by tramways) followed by the railways (which invariably reached right up to the pit head) and, most recently, the introduction of the large motorised coal lorries and the modern road network, have all played their part in overcoming this problem.

The coming of the canals was a mixed blessing to the Warwickshire mine owners. The canal reached Atherstone, but it was over twenty years before it proceeded past Atherstone to join up with the canals further north, during which time there was a lot of legal bickering. It was later realised that Atherstone coal owners, who were also canal shareholders, had been the cause of the controversy. It would appear that they wanted the canals to take their coal away, but not the coal of their competitors further north.

Their fears seem to have been justified as, when the canal systems were joined up, the south Staffordshire coalfield could produce coal and transport it to Warwickshire more cheaply than it could be produced in Warwickshire - thanks to the more advantageous conditions pertaining in south Staffordshire with its shallow, level, dry, gas-free seams. But there they worked the very wasteful 'bord and pillar' system, where only forty per-cent of the coal was extracted, as opposed to the more efficient 'longwall system' employed in Warwicks. The result was that around the 1870s, the south Staffordshire seams started becoming exhausted. At a stroke, Warwickshire had not only lost its keenest competitor, it had also gained a market - all the Black Country industries that had built up dependent on Staffordshire coal. Also, skilled miners were available to man the expanding Warwickshire field. So, Exhall Pit was opened in 1857, Birchmoor in 1860, Amington in 1863, Birch Coppice in 1875, Alvecote in 1877, Ansley in 1878, Griff Clara in 1891, and Kingsbury in 1894. Arley and Newdigate opened in 1901. Ten major new pits in little over forty years!

Another fillip to the Baddesley mining scene was when a family of mining entrepeneurs from the Nuneaton area, the Stratford family, bought the Merevale estate from the Devereaux's. The Devereaux's had held it since the Dissolution of 1538, when Henry VIII had the monastery closed. The Stratfords lost little time in acquiring land and mining rights in Baddesley and in upper Grendon, leasing the Riddings and Grendon Wood pits to Messrs Burslem and England on terms most advantageous to themselves. As weighing machines had not as yet been introduced the amount of coal being produced was measured in stacks, all coal produced being piled into stacks (the stack size being pre-determined) for the estate's bailiff to count.

The estate worked in the area between Baddesley Wood, Coppice Corner and Lower House Lane, sinking their first shaft near the Penmire Brook in 1734. Also the seam of limestone along the western boundary of the parish, in the vicinity of Garratt's Lane (better known as 'Sludgy Lane') was worked.

By 1780 the situation had changed. The canal, after years and years of wrangling during which time the canal had reached no further than the Coleshill Road basin in Atherstone, had extended through Atherstone and connected up with the canal network to the north. And so reached a position where it was possible to transport Baddesley coal cheaply to most of the country. The Watling Street had been turnpiked, and a canal wharf had been put in alongside the Watling Street at Whittington. An early tramway was extended to the wharf, to take coal from the Merevale pits. Another was put in to transport coal from Baddesley to the Watling Street.

A further change was that Richard Geast (later Dugdale) had become the major Lord of the Manor of Baddesley, and so had greater access to land for mining purposes in the manor. He had also married into the Stratford family, so that the mining expertise of that family was available to him.

Banbury Pits

The ability to transport coal relatively cheaply by the canals attracted a syndicate of Banbury coal factors who, in 1790, leased an old mine in the vicinity of Baddesley Wood, and laid in a tramway from it to the Watling Street, whence it was carted to the wharf, then by canal to Banbury. They must have found it worth while, as they went on to sink and work five other pits nearby.

Old Church Pits

A few years later Mr Dugdale opened the Old Brickat mine, the spoilbank of which may still be seen at the rear of No 132, St Nicholas Estate. This must have been a fairly long-lived pit, as it is shown on Dumolo's map of 1848 as still being served by a branch of the Black Path tramway. He used part of the Banbury merchants' tramway to serve this, when it first opened. This ran down the rear of the St Nicholas Estate, and is now the AE25 footpath, in front of what used to be Baddesley Wood, reaching the Watling Street at the rear of Penmire Close. Penmire Close, formerly Lower Baddesley, being the site of Dugdale's offices and stocking ground.

Old Brickat proved to be the first of what became known as the three Old Church Pits. The second was at the dirt mound on the Low Common, which is popularly known as the Bunnybank or Rabbit Bank for obvious reasons. This was opened in 1791, and was 90 yards deep to work the Ryder seam (6 feet 4 inches thick at that point) but, according to old mining maps, it descended dab in the middle of an arrow-head-shaped local fault. To serve it the tramway was turned northward along the line of the present AE50 footpath.

The third Old Church Pit was sunk in 1805, adjacent to the entrance to the old churchyard, astride the road from Hill Top past the old church, which used to carry on past the church to Lower House Lane, now the AE49 footpath. The pit did not last very long. Water broke in from the roof and the workings had to be abandoned. However, during the life of the pit, the tramway was extended across Low Common to serve it.

Waterloo Pit

The tramway also branched southwards, along Hill Top, past the existing church gates, across the church fields to the Waterloo Pit, the site of which was on the opposite side of the road to Church House. As one might expect the Waterloo Pit was opened in 1815, the year that Wellington defeated Napoleon at Waterloo. A matter of interest, the shaft of this pit was not filled in when the pit ceased operating, but was left open and used as a well. It was still open and in use as such when the water mains were first laid round the village in 1902. This would appear to indicate that Waterloo pit must have had problems with water.

Jim Crow's Pit

In 1817, the tramway was extended across the common to serve Jim Crow's Pit. This was sited sixty or seventy yards south of the vicarage gates, alongside the Black Path. To reach it the tramway passed from the Waterloo Pit, in front of the Crow Hill cottages, and alongside the vicarage.

Jim Crow's pit was commonly known as the 'Paling Pit', as it used to have a square fence or palings round it, until the shaft collapsed in the 1950s and had to be topped up. Usual practice was to lay timber baulks across a shaft approximately eighty feet down when the pit was closed, and fill up the eighty feet above. It was a common occurrence for such shafts to collapse when the timber baulks rotted through. This happened at the Maypole Pit as well as at Jim Crow's, and quite a few other unnamed pits as well. When the Maypole Pit shaft collapsed in the 1950s, the National Coal Board (who had inherited the responsibility for such pits) topped up the shaft and put a raft of concrete over the top. The concrete raft is still visible, a few yards behind the winding wheel memorial.

The Hene Pits

There were three shafts at these pits which opened in 1816, according to an old freelance mining engineer's mining map of the area. They were sited at Hill Top, in the field adjacent to 'The Cottage' (better known to the older residents as 'Jody Woods Cottage'). The embankment of the tramway which served both the Hene pits and the later Engine and Bye pits may still be seen crossing the field immediately behind 'The Cottage', to join the other tramways at the Old Brickat.

The Million Guinea Road

Soon after 1817 an underground haulage road was put in. This ran roughly parallel to the later Black Path haulage way on the surface, connecting the third of the Old Church pits, the Hene pits, the Maypole and Waterloo pits and also Jim Crow's pit. It travelled under the whole length of the common to a shaft in the Merevale fields adjacent to the Colliery Farm, known as Reuben's Wind. Apparently all coal produced in Baddesley travelled underground to Reuben's Wind where it was wound to the surface. From there the coal was taken on a tramway which ran alongside Waste Lane (more commonly known as 'Folly Lane') to the wharf.

This tramway had been built in 1795 to serve the Merevale pits. This made redundant all the Baddesley surface tramways which, until that time, had taken coal to a stocking ground at Lower Baddesley. Spontaneous combustion caused an underground fire at Reuben's Wind in 1832 which made the shaft inoperable. The Black Path tramway and its tunnel were put in as an alternative.

Engine and Bye pits

These two shafts opened around 1830, immediately adjacent to the three shafts of the Hene pits. The Engine pit was for a steam pumping engine, and the Bye pit a winding shaft using a horse gin. Family records show that the engineer at the pumping engine was John Collins, licenseee at the old Black Horse Inn, Ball's Road (now Newlands Road), Baddesley. This pumping engine finished working in 1848.

The Black Path

This is shown on a mining map of 1845, labelled 'Railway' (as, for that matter, is the underground 'Million Guinea Road'). The name Black Path is much later as, over the years of bearing coal, spillage had given it a surface layer of coal slack.

Until the 1930s many local tradesmen used horses in their businesses, and also quite a few other parishioners owned horses, horses and traps being popular and a status symbol. Most of these horses grazed on the

Original stone block from the Black Path tramway with replica rail.
Recreated and photographed by John Nunn.

common, keeping the common well grazed off. They would pay for a 'grazing right', entitling them to graze their horses on the common. As a result there were no long grasses on the common, and tree and shrub seedlings could not get established. Then the Black Path was a wide track, often used by coal carts bearing miners' allowance coal from the colliery. It became overgrown as it is today when the common ceased to be grazed by horses. Horse-drawn transport had been replaced by motor transport, and the horse-drawn coal carts given way to coal lorries.

Black Path tramway had been put in, in the 1830s, as an emergency measure, after Reuben's Wind burned out, as there was no means of transporting Baddesley coal to the wharfe. It stretched from the Bunnybank to the tunnel on the common. The tunnel is 430 yards long and emerges in the fields on the Merevale side of Folly Lane. To get the tunnel driven as quickly as possible, a shaft was sunk approximately half way along it to enable four faces to be worked instead of the usual one from each end. From there the tramway joined the one laid in 1795 from the Merevale pits to the wharf. It passed through a further two tunnels at the lower end, where the track turned away from the lane.

The tramway was of the Coalbrookdale type, using plates six feet long, which would probably best be described today as heavy duty angle irons. There were no sleepers, the plates joined by chairs mounted on stone, fish-tail-shaped blocks, each weighing 67 lbs [30kg], let into the ground. This type of tramway was in common use all over the country. One unusual feature was that, instead of using worked sandstone or limestone blocks, Mr Dugdale used fired clay blocks, probably fired in his own brick kilns at Little Brum. Several specimens are available, but when two blocks were used every two yards, it means that there was a block for every yard of the tramways length. There must be hundreds of these blocks lying around just below the surface. The iron wheels had a flat rim, and ran between the two uprights of the 'angle iron' plates.

The subject of tramways in Baddesley is a fascinating one. There were tramways in Baddesley for the whole of the period that tramways were in use nationally, but there is little documentary evidence on the types of rails or plates and wheels used, except for the Black Path. The one in the Riddings was so early that there can be little doubt that it used wooden rails and wheels.

Some time was spent finding the lines of some tramways. By accident, it was discovered that by using dowsing techniques it is possible to detect each individual line of rails or plates, the gauge of the track and where

Stationary Haulage Engine
on the Black Path

The stationary engine
on the Black Path.

69

crossings were. This can be done even though the rails have been removed for nearly a century and a half, or the ground has been disturbed by ploughing. But excavation or opencast coal working makes them undetectable. It seems that this is commonly known by dowsers and is referred to as 'remanence'. If, for instance, a metal object, such as a hammer, is laid on the ground and then removed, a dowser, using metal dowsing rods, can detect where the hammer has lain.

The stretch between the church gates and the tunnel had the trams drawn along by an endless chain, driven by a low pressure beam rotative stationary haulage engine, sited near the spot where the Day of Praise services are held. Steam was supplied by an onion-shaped boiler, the type first used by Newcomen, on his Fire Engine. The rectangular pool supplying water, known as the 'Bottom Rezzer' (reservoir), was popular with children for its frogs spawn and newts. It was filled in during the 1930s with household refuse, chiefly ashes, when the Parish Council was responsible for disposing of refuse and desperate for places in which to dump. Several other old reservoirs were filled in on the common around that time - Jim Crow's, the 'Middle Rezzer', and the Maypole Pool - as well as other interesting pits and hollows around the parish, also relics of industrial activity, such as quarries and limestone diggings.

We have a fair idea of what the haulage engine looked like, as it is depicted in Van Nieman's painting 'Mr Dugdales Coalworks on Baddesley Common', owned by Sir William. For much of its life it was driven by a woman, described as 'a pipe smoking, pit-brow woman' named Emma McCreath. A Londoner, she came to Baddesley with her husband. After his death she married a Mr Chetwynd. She later married again, this time to my great-grandfather, William Fretwell, by that time a widower. Following his death she returned to London. A slightly less derogatory description of her was given by a contemporary, a lay preacher and fellow elder of the Congregational church, in a sermon, in which he described her as an example to be followed. He maintained that she worked hard for the church and for the women of the village, and was very much missed when she returned to London. On the subject of her smoking a pipe, he said that she only did it once as a result of a dare.

Little Brum

There were four shafts in this area, but no record is to hand of their dates. All that is known is that two of them were working the Seven Foot

70

seam at a depth of 86 yards. There was also a clay factory there with its kilns. It owes its name to the fact that, with its colliery steam raising plants and brick kilns, it was likened to a Little Brummagem, Little Brum. A tramway was put in to serve the pits and factory.

Most of the waste material from mining at Baddesley was claystone. Rather than buying material to line the pit shafts, the claystone was used to produce bricks for the purpose. Bricks were also produced for sale, tiles too, and (as mentioned) tramway blocks.

Maypole Pit

This was sited on the opposite side of the road to the Maypole Inn, the mound there being the pit spoilbank. The up-cast shaft was an adit or drift emerging at the surface on the Ridding footpath, alongside the site of the present electrical power sub-station. Sinking commenced in June 1829, and finished in November in the same year, 70 yards deep in the Seven Feet seam. It worked just one face, a longwall advancing face, which started working under the edge of the Quaker burial ground, reaching from the Infants' School, to a point near the church gates, and worked back uphill towards the basset. This was probably to cause the water to drain away from the workings, and allow tubs (underground versions of trams) to be drawn to and from the face by means of a gravity haulage, or in local parlance, a 'jig'. This finished work in 1851, just inside Grendon Wood, having passed under the Red Lion pub in 1848.

Speedwell Pit

When sunk this was known as 'The New Pit'. It was sunk adjacent to a water shaft sunk in 1824, possibly a drainage adit from the Hene pits. Prior to Speedwell, all Baddesley pits had been sunk just to the west of the basset and had worked the coal not covered by the water bearing layers. But Speedwell was a departure from past practices. It was a 'keel pit', that is, it was sunk down through the water beds, with a sump as a water reservoir at the bottom of the shaft - the first time this had been done in Warwickshire. The great strides made in pumping engine design probably made this feasible.

Sinking commenced in March 1847 and went down 90 yards before three sets of 'tubbing' were inserted, in addition to the brick lining, to contain the water. 'Tubbing' is cast iron segments which, when bolted together form a watertight tube, in this case eight feet in diameter. At 183 yards and one inch,

The old Maypole Inn.

on Friday February 16th 1849, the top of the Rider seam was reached, this seam being five feet four inches thick, below which was six inches of 'pricking', then three feet seven inches of Barecoal, locally pronounced 'bakel'. In August 1849, at 232 yards and a half inch, the top of the Seven Feet seam appeared, this being exactly six feet thick. And at 251 yards two feet and three and a half inches, in the sump, the final curb was laid, bricked up and sinking finished on September 15th 1849. The last sinking payment was 'Paid to J.Evans & Co 12yrds @ 60/- by bargain or £36-0-0. Sept 20th 1849'.

Speedwell was notable in another respect too. It was the second pit ever to be equipped with pit cages. This entailed fitting two pitch pine guides, one on each side of the shaft for the whole of its depth. These engaged a bracket fitted each side of the cage, to prevent it rotating in the shaft. Before this coal had been wound to the surface in big buckets, called 'hoppits' or 'skips'. The coal coming to the bottom of the shaft in tubs had to be unloaded and the coal transferred to the hoppit. Any dirt accidentally loaded into the tubs was put back into them to be taken back to the coalface. But, using cages, the tubs went on to the cage and were wound to the surface before being unloaded. The result was that pit spoilbanks, which had previously consisted mainly of refuse from shaft sinking, now were added to daily with dirt wound to the surface in the tubs.

The winding engine was a beam steam engine, with a twelve-inch diameter cylinder, built into the engine house, with the brickwork supporting the various shafts, etc. The winding rope used was a four-inch flattened hemp rope. The engine was named 'Sampson' and in its later days was used as a capstan for lifting parts of the Harriet Ella pump during repairs etc. Sampson was still standing until the 1950s, but had fallen into a corroded state of disrepair and was replaced by a more modern steam engine during World War I.

The New Pit or Speedwell Pit landsale was sited at Hill Top and coal was drawn up to it by a stationary steam haulage engine along a tramway, using a track in the church fields, now the footpath AE62. At the upper end of the footpath one may still see the embankment of this tramway. The landsale was known as the Londin Gates landsale, 'londin' being a corruption of 'landing' which, in pit parlance, is a place where tubs come to rest, after being drawn up an incline. Coal for local use was sold at the landsale, but the greater part of Speedwell's coal was transported along the Black Path tramway, on its way to the wharf.

However, on March 27th 1861, the workings of the later Stratford Pit, a mile away to the south, 'thurled through' (joined together underground) to the Speedwell workings. This made it possible for the Speedwell coal to be transported underground and wound up to the surface at the Stratford pits.

A party was held, on April 1st 1861, to which most of the employees were invited. This coincided with Mr Dugdale's 61st birthday. A number of toasts were proposed; one of these mentioned the fact that a pumping engine was ordered, to be installed at Speedwell, and that a water course was to be constructed, to drain the two pits. The Scottish contractors, who had driven the roadway between the two pits, were also congratulated. It was also mentioned that a new railway was to be built, meaning the narrow gauge railway from the Stratford pits to the wharf, to take the combined product of Speedwell and Stratford. Also mentioned was a clay crushing mill, probably a pug-mill (pug-mills inceased the quality of clay for bricks and tiles). One must suppose that this was intended for one of Mr Dugdale's brick factories, probably the one at Little Brum.

The account of the party is in rhyme, and it reads that the Scots workmen driving the head between the two pits encountered faults which had to be driven through, slowing their progress, and had some trouble in making the deadline to enable the planned party to take place. The author of the rhyming account likened their achievement to the Relief of Lucknow, the 'Black Hole of Calcutta', during the Indian Mutiny a few years before, when Scottish troops

Sampson winding engine, Speedwell Pit, c.1849

74

led by pipers relieved a number of people who were imprisoned in a small room.

Speedwell coal was the last coal to be transported along the Black Path on its way to the wharf, all the other Baddesley Colieries pits having expired. So the commons tramways came to a halt in 1861. When the pumping staion station started up, needing coal for its steam raising plant, the Black Path came into operation again, this time taking coal in the opposite direction, from Stratford pits to Speedwell. Until 1878, when the Kingsbury Mineral Spur Line came into operation, this passed alongside the Speedwell pit, so that coal could be dropped off to supply Speedwell. This operation was known in the village as 'slack emptying' and done on Saturday afternoons, when several truckloads of small coal were emptied alongside Speedwell pit for use in the boilers there.

The Camp Meeting

Until the late 1920s, once a year, early on a summer Sunday morning, a religious service was held on the piece of ground known as the 'Londin' Gates'. Details of its origin are lost in time. It is believed to commemorate several women being killed in a pit accident on a Sunday. One old miner told the tale that an owner's son, one Sunday morning during the school holidays, took some guests, young men and young women, horse riding on Baddesley Common. They came to one of the Hill Top pits, where he demonstrated his ability to operate the winding mechanism. He lowered some of the lads to the bottom of the shaft, then went on to lower some of the girls, but lost control, with the result that some of the girls were killed. There is nothing to substantiate the story, but the Camp Meetings took place, and it was always considered unlucky for women to go down Baddesley pits.

Mr Hombrey's Pit

In a Parliament report of 1840, mention is made of a small pit, in a wood, operated by a horse gin, and employing thirteen people. This was the four-feet diameter shaft, in the spinney, alongside the Watery Lane, at the bottom of the second hill. A Mr Hombrey was running it.

There are quite a few other shafts in the parish. In a child's exercise book, written up by Mr Pogmore, there are records of shafts sunk by the Baddesley Collieries, a different shaft on each page, with all sorts of details, dates, depths etc. The problem is that there is scant information as to their location.

Kingsbury Mineral Spur

In the latter half of the nineteenth century, pits were being sunk through the water-bearing layers of the Warwickshire field, that is, away to the west from the banana-shaped traditional coalfield stretching from Coventry through Nuneaton to Tamworth. In the early 1870s, Birch Coppice or Hall End Pit was being sunk and plans were afoot to bring a mineral spur from the Derby to Birmingham line at Kingsbury, to serve the proposed pit. The Dugdale family got in on the scheme and arranged to have the line extended to serve the Stratford Pits also. The Enabling Act was passed on July 28th 1872.

The contractor to build the line was a John Perkins. His first job was to buy all the land that the proposed line would cover. One of the lots of land affected was a smallholding, on the Parkside, in the vicinity of what is now Perkins' Bridge. Having purchased the smallholding, John Perkins used it as his residence whilst the Spur Line was being built, until the smallholding was finally buried by the railway's embankment. It is said that John Perkins' son courted one of Gabriel Collins' three spinster daughters (of No. 1 Newlands Road). The smallholding's orchard (which was not buried), was known as Perkins' Orchard, and the bridge built on the site, over the Parkside Road, was known as Perkins' Bridge.

On February 2nd 1878, the new spur line was opened and put to use. It lasted 111 years, until the Stratford Pits (later Baddesley Mine) closed. The last load of thirty thirty-three ton tankers passed down en route to Didcot Power Station on January 28th 1989.

The benefits of having access to a main railway line must have been considered satisfactory, as a few years later in 1885 the colliery bought a loco and had a connection put in on the main Crewe to Euston line. This is not surprising as much of the 'Best Baddesley Ryder Cobbles' were sold in London and the South Coast, this being a very high quality household coal, with a high calorific content and a low ash content. It was traditionally popular with the canal boating fraternity transporting it.

A little story I can't resist telling. During World War II I served in the Royal Navy. After an operation we returned to Britain, to our base at Lee on Solent. While I was there my family informed me that another Baddesley miner, Bill 'Cog' Sweet, had joined the Royal Navy, and was stationed nearby, so I contacted him. He was in training at H.M.S Collingwood, a naval establishment near Fareham. It was arranged that we should meet at Fareham

The Kingsbury Mineral Spur viaduct with one of the last run-of-mine trains to leave Baddesley Colliery, en route to Dicot power station. Behind the locomotive would be thirty wagons each weighing thirty-three tons. Photo taken 28th January 1989 by John Nunn and reproduced with kind permission.

bus station, and, arriving there first I positioned myself on the opposite side of the street to enable me to watch both bus station entrances. He arrived and came over, accusing me of 'picking my spot', indicating the shop behind me that I had not noticed. It was a large double-fronted shop, with two bay windows, decorated in all white lace, with a large glass bowl in each bay, each filled with coal cobbles, labelled 'Best Baddesley Ryder Cobbles'.

The Mineral Spur Line from Kingsbury was only used once to convey passengers. On Saturday December 12th 1964 a train of twelve coach-loads of trainspotters travelled up the line to the pit. They wanted to look at the old Beyer Garret articulated steam locomotive, which had been at work at the colliery from new in 1937 and was one of the few of its type left in the country. However, the pit manager, a Mr Hughes, refused them permission to view the old loco, and they were sent away disappointed.

One of the more spectacular features of the Mineral Spur line is the viaduct over the valley of the Sugar Brook, in the vicinity of the Watery Lane Ford ('the paddle'). Being the biggest gap in the railway embankment, it has been used as a route for the large-diameter sewage pipes then, more recently, for the two large-diameter high-pressure gas pipes, conveying gas from the north to the south of the country.

Merevale Pits

There were pits at Merevale probably before there any at Baddesley. It has been established that the Merevale monks used coal. With the advent of the Stratfords, then the Dugdales, Merevale was owned by them. Before the canal became available for transporting their product, a tramway brought the coal from the pits near Colliery Farm to Folly Lane, where presumably it was loaded on to carts for transport to the Watling Street. In 1795, this was extended down to the wharf, passing through two tunnels, then crossing the Watling by way of a level crossing. When all Baddesley Coal was transported underground and wound up Reubens Wind, this tramway increased in importance, becoming a two line affair, empty trams up, full trams down.

When Reubens Wind burned itself out the tramway was diverted to the Merevale end of the common tunnel to receive the trams from the Black Path. At this time the tramway was of the Coalbrookdale type, but it is not known what types the preceding ones were. At one stage it was proposed that the level of the tramway be lifted to enable the trams to cross the Watling over a bridge.

With the opening of the Stratford pits, the tramway was re-routed to serve it; after the thurl through to Speedwell, in 1861, all Baddesley coal was wound up Stratford Pits. Baddesley Colliery's eggs were in one basket. So, a narrow gauge railway was installed from the wharf to the Stratford pits, despite a proposal that a standard 4ft 8ins gauge line be put in, which would have entailed throwing open the lower two tunnels. Using a narrow gauge railway meant that any coal not transferred to canal barges had to be transhipped to standard gauge wagons at the wharf, to be taken on to the nearby Euston to Crewe line, as a connection and sidings had opened on July 8th 1871.

The Kingsbury Mineral Spur had been put to work in 1878 and, of course, this was standard gauge, so that the colliery surface was having to contend with the two different gauges. In 1885 it was decided to throw open the two tunnels and change to standard gauge. As it was a private line this meant using their own locomotive. A 15.5 ton 0-4-0 Hunslett saddle tanked locomotive was decided on. They had the manufacturers modify one from the original design, to suit their needs. One of the modifications was a cab to cover the driver and fireman. Delivery was accepted on June 1st 1885 and the £1,350 it cost paid in instalments.

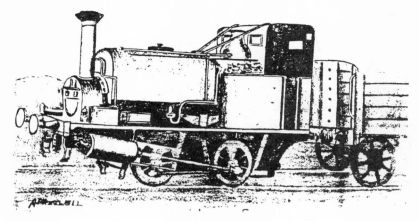

The first locomotive purchased by the colliery in 1885,
a Hunslett saddle-tank 0-4-0..

The Beyer Garrett locomotive

Over the years quite a number of locos were owned by the colliery, but the best known and most famous one was the Beyer Garrett. This was purchased new in 1937 and named 'William Francis'. It was a smaller version of a design popular in South and East Africa, where, even today, one can see trains of wagons nearly half-a-mile long being hauled by monstrous Beyer Garrets. They were designed to contend with steep inclines and sharp bends, being virtually two engines in one, having an engine at each end with the boiler slung between the two.

William Francis was arguably the last Beyer Garrett in use in this country, and generated a great deal of interest in the train spotter circles. It continued in use until the early 1960s when, like every other steam locomotive, it had to go, to make way for more efficient diesel and diesel-electric locos. It stood idle in the pit loco sheds for a couple of years, before going away. During this time it was a continuous source of pilgrimages by train spotters.

The Beyer Garrett left the colliery shortly afterwards. At the time, it was understood to have been bought by the Canadian Locomotive Museum, and was to be transported there. But a few years later it appeared at the Bressingham Museum, at Diss in Norfolk, where it still is. However it now has

The Beyer Garrett locomotive, now in Bressingham Museum.

a brown livery, whereas all its working life it was dark blue, and none of the numbers on it today bear any relation to the manufacturer's, the owner's or the Coal Board numbers it used to wear.

Not until its last decade or so at the pit did anyone realise that the engine was anything out of the ordinary. Prior to that it was simply known as 'the articulated'. It was admirably suited for the inclined line down to the wharf and to the sharp curves of the confined pit yard.

Harriet Ella

After the Speedwell pit and the Stratford pit had connected together below ground, it was decided to drain surplus water from the workings of the combined pits to Speedwell. To raise it to the surface a huge steam pump was obtained from Thornewill and Warham's and was erected at the top of the shaft. Named 'Harriet Ella', the engine had a stroke of ten feet, and a seven feet diameter vertical cylinder. This operated a massive wrought iron beam which rested on the front wall of the engine house. Steam at 20 p.s.i. [1.4 bar] was produced by four Cornish Boilers. The beam in turn operated a 243 yard long pitch pine rod, 22 by 15 inches thick, with six pumps attached. The lowest, at the bottom of the shaft was a force pump, with five ram pumps spaced at intervals above it, the upper one being 150 feet below the surface. It

The Speedwell pumping station. The small beam engine on the left was the original winding engine of 1849. The central building was the Harriet Ella pumping engine. On the right is the more recent modern winding engine.

made four down strokes per minute and at every stroke, each pump delivered 110 gallons to the pump above it, the upper pump delivering to the surface. The water delivered to the surface ran over the condenser, to give increased efficiency, and on to a reservoir. In the process the water became warm, to the delight of the local children, who paddled in the ford and swam in the reservoir. Warm water in the reservoir, and the overflow, flowed into the Watery Lane ford, 'the paddle', which was also warm when the pump was working. The pump operated for eight hours each day.

The pump was used until the early 1950s, when it was replaced by a more modern, more efficient, electrically-operated submersible pump, lowered into the shaft. To operate the electric pump power lines had to be brought across the fields to it. The power line was extended to the village, to a transformer in the allotments in Speedwell Lane (now the site of the old peoples' bungalows and council houses), and gave a second power supply for the village. The village had been suffering from a lack of power at the time, having until then only one feed into it. This caused all kinds of difficulties in the homes, especially with the newly-introduced television sets.

Chapter 5

The Stratford Pit Disaster

Stratford Pit proved to be the longest-lived of all the Baddesley Collieries pits. When all of the others had been closed, its original name became disused, to be known as Baddesley Collieries. But to locals it was always known as Baxterley Pit, or more commonly still, just 'Baxt'ley'.

There were two seven-feet diameter shafts, 33 feet apart with the winding engine in line with them, east and west. The first sod was cut by Mrs Harriet Dugdale at 2 p.m. on May 1st 1851. The shafts were sunk on what was Baxterley Greater Common - there being two commons in Baxterley, this one and the Lesser Common, usually called Wigston Hill Common. Both were enclosed by Mr Dugdale in an Act of 1865 (this being the last enclosure act in Warwickshire).

The shafts were sunk down through the water-bearing layers, as had been done at Speedwell, to a depth of 280 yards. The shaft linings were red brick for forty yards. Then there was 70 yards of cast iron tubbing, another 30 yards of brick, a second 35 yard length of tubbing, then brickwork to the bottom. All this passed through a two feet six inches layer of limestone, the Four Feet seam of coal (four feet four inches thick here) at 226 yards and two feet, beyond was 8 feet 6 inches of Rider, with 9 inches of 'bat' or 'pricking', then 5 feet 6 inches of Barecoal at 246 yards and two feet. Below this were three feet of Ell coal at 266 yards and two feet, the two feet and eight inches thick Smithy seam at 280 yards, finally the five feet six inches band of Seven Feet coal. There were, and still are, several other seams below that.

The two shafts were known in the early days as the 'wet' and the 'dry' shafts, the wet shaft being the upcast shaft. Forty yards down the upcast shaft, a nine feet by six feet drift led to a 40 yard deep fan shaft. Later, after a third, 14 feet diameter, shaft had been sunk, they became No.'s 1 and 2 shafts. Two pitch pine cage guide rods were used, as at Speedwell, and were still in use when the pit closed in 1989.

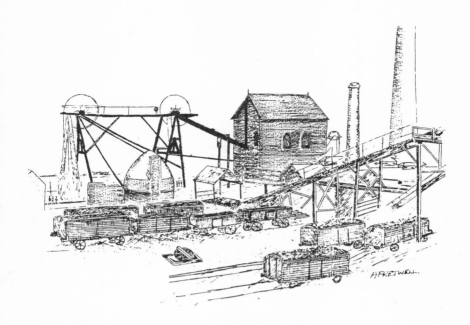

Stratford Pit c.1890.

There was no means of transmitting power underground, beyond the main haulage road which was served by an endless steel rope, operated by a steam haulage engine located near the bottom of the shaft. The steam was fed from boilers on the surface, and piped down the upcast shaft. So the coal faces always worked up the slope of the seams, to enable gravity haulages to be used, that is, the weight of the full tubs running down from the faces pulled the empty tubs up - generally known as gravity haulages, but locally as 'jigs'.

Horses were used in awkward places. Seventeen of them were in use in the pit in 1882. These only came up from the mine when the pit was closed for a few days. Mention can be found of them being brought to the surface for Grendon Wakes in 1871. Another note in the same year states, 'George Hall crushed while jigging at No 5 stall, doctor sent for.'

A steam winding engine, embossed with the name 'Stratford', was purpose built by Thornewill and Wareham, having a single vertical cylinder 32 inches in diameter, with a six foot stroke. The 13 feet diameter winding drum was mounted above it, borne by the massive masonary walls of the engine-house. This winding engine remained in use for over a century, until around 1954, when it was planned to sink the larger 14 feet diameter No.3

shaft a further 600 feet and to wind the sinking debris to the surface up the two older shafts, to prevent interference with production. A more efficient electric winder was installed, to deal with the increased amount of work envisaged.

Draining 'made' water

The seams were steeply inclined, from east to west, and wet to work. After a thurl was made through to Speedwell, a road with a water course was driven through in such a manner that it followed the Two Yard or Ryder seam along the lower boundary of the workings, and maintaining a steady fall or gradient to Speedwell, one and a quarter miles away to the north. It passed within approximately four hundred yards of the shafts, catching naturally (or being arranged to accept) all of the surplus water 'made' in the pit, and draining it to Speedwell. To raise this water to the surface, Speedwell was converted into a pumping station, by installing a huge pumping engine named 'Harriet Ella', also built by Thornewill and Wareham, in 1868.

This system of having a water course along the lower edge of the workings, known as 'The Water Level', into which any water could be made to drain, seems to have been considered a success. Water from all the pits' extensive workings were pumped to the water level, until the 1980s when a large water lodgement was made near the pit bottom, into which the water level was drained. Speedwell remained in operation until the 1960s when large electrically-operated turbine pumps lifted water up the No. 3 shaft, in seven-inch diameter pipes, making the Speedwell pumping station redundant.

The underground boiler

During the 1870s, the coal extraction (at the time known as the Deep Workings) proceeded down the inclined seam, past and lower than the Water Level. A consultant mining engineer from Derby, named Mr Gillett, devised a scheme to drive another water course along the newer bottom boundary, the Deep Boundary. This would be a matter of nine hundred yards from the shaft bottom, so that surplus water could be made to drain into it. And the water was to be bailed by buckets into tubs, which in turn were drawn up the haulage road to the Speedwell water level. But water spillage from the tubs damaged the haulage road, and the system was very labour intensive. So Mr Gillett arranged to have a pump installed, to pump the water from the new water course to the Speedwell Water Level, so that water also could drain to Speedwell.

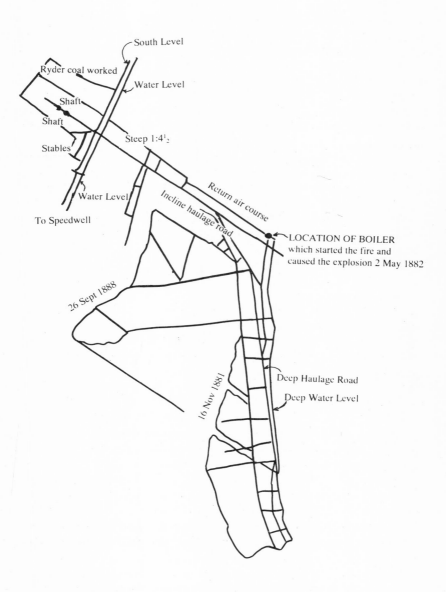

South Level

Ryder coal worked

Water Level

Shaft

Shaft

Steep 1:4½

Stables

Water Level

To Speedwell

Incline haulage road

Return air course

LOCATION OF BOILER
which started the fire and
caused the explosion 2 May 1882

26 Sept 1888

16 Nov 1881

Deep Haulage Road

Deep Water Level

85

A steam pump was installed in February 1882, powered by steam piped from the surface boilers, and an extension of the steam pipe feeding the pit bottom steam haulage engine. This was not successful. Baddesley, like all other Warwickshire pits, was then considered gas free. This meant that the miners worked by candle light, 'naked flame' lighting - the men suplying their own candles, of course. So a boiler was obtained from Thornewell and Wareham and installed in the return airway, adjacent to the pump. A facsimile of the drawing supplied by Thornewell's, by way of installation instructions, is shown.

Unfortunately, the hot flue gases emitting from this came into contact with coal in the roof. The furnace started a fire in the roof coal near the mouth of the boiler funnel almost as soon as the boiler was started up on April 14th 1882. The heat caused several falls of coal and clot on to the boiler, breaking the funnel which had to be mended. It had become the practice to throw water from a bucket on to the red hot roof coal. Then the manager, Mr Parker, had a hose attached to the pump which was used to spray the hot area. This would blacken the surface for a short time.

Disaster stikes Dugdale's pit

The boiler's furnace had not been alight for several shifts and men had been doing repairs to the boiler. They had reported to Parker on the serviceability of it but had failed to mention the patch of glowing coal in the roof near the chimney.

At four o'clock on the afternoon of May 1st, a fourteen year old boy named Thomas Shilton sneaked through the thurl to look at the boiler, which he had never seen. When questioned at the enquiry, he said that he had seen the patch of glowing coal in the roof. When asked how big it was he said 'as big as the top of a bucket'. And this was after the furnace had been raked out and unlit for several shifts, because of the repair work.

On the afternoon of Monday May 1st 1882, senior pit deputy, Charles Day, completed his pre-shift underground examination and was making his way up the incline towards the pit bottom. He met the night shift which, due to the pit being at play, only consisted of eight married men and a boy, who had come on shift at six o'clock. Mr Day stopped to discuss their work for the

Opposite: *Baddesley Colliery Deep Workings in the Ryder seam. 'A' marks the location of the boiler and engine which started the fire and caused the explosion on May 2nd 1882.*

86

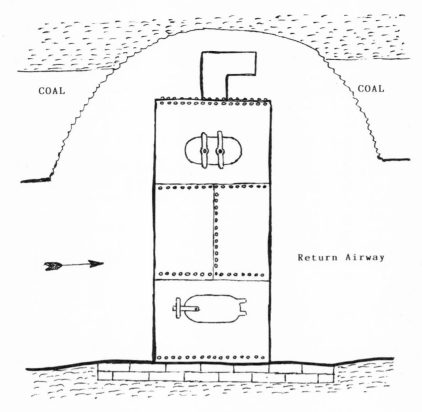

COAL

COAL

Return Airway

Sketch showing the position of the boiler in the mine.

shift. They told him that Parker wanted them to dint (lower) a length of rails, several hundred yards inbye (towards the coal face) of the steam pump. After some thought Day told them how to proceed. He took Bill Blower up the incline to fetch a horse, then they went back down to fetch Joseph Orton and some tubs for the dirt.

Two of the men, John Ross and another, had stopped on the surface to send timber into the pit. The deputy told these to go into the workings, when they had finished handling the timber. Mr Day's son, the night shift deputy, shifted him at ten o'clock and remarked about smoke in the upcast shaft. When he rode up the shaft Mr Day had to put his scarf in his mouth, because of the smoke and fumes, so he went back down the downcast shaft, to try to warn the night shift, but could not get anywhere near them. He was met at the top of the haulage road with a wall of smoke.

A number of pitmen, and officials living nearby, came to the pit and descended to join in the attempts to reach the nine nightshift men, including two more of Mr Day's sons. Obviously an air door was open, by-passing the ventilation system, allowing smoke from the return airway to back up into the main airway. The main haulage road was full of smoke to within a foot from the floor, where there was a strong passage of air. They erected a series of makeshift wooden frames covered in non-inflammable fabric (a common pit practice), with an aperture at the top, forcing the air flow along the roof, clearing the roadway behind of smoke. Then they moved on to erect another.

Rowland Till, the carpenter, was just nailing fabric to the last frame erected, when a coal dust explosion occurred. Everyone was injured or burned, to a greater or lesser extent, the atmosphere having become a poisonous mix of smoke and carbonic acid gas and the only breathable air was at ground level.

There were thirty-three rescuers in the pit when the coal dust explosion occurred early on Tuesday morning, including Mr Dugdale, the mine owner; Mr Pogmore, his agent; his son, Mr Frank Pogmore, a solicitor; and Mr Reuben Smallman, a mining engineer from Nuneaton; Charles Day; and a number of the other local miners. They had only been in the pit a few minutes when the explosion occurred, Charles Day was fortunate in as much that, being perturbed at the numbers entering the pit he went back to the onsetter, to stop any more men descending, while the rest of the party went on inbye.

Day was talking to the onsetter when the explosion took place. He was hurled off his feet and lost his lamp. Some of the party made their way back to the surface, most of them badly burned and suffering badly with the effects of fumes inhalation. All three of Mr Day's sons were affected. A number of doctors arrived and treated the casualties, before sending them to their homes in vehicles. One of those who failed to get out of the pit was Mr Dugdale.

By nine o'clock the Inspector of Mines, Mr Stokes, had arrived on the scene, as had Mr Spruce, a mining engineer from Tamworth, together with his assistant, Mr Mottram, and the undermanager of Birch Coppice colliery, Mr Marsh. After some preparation, these four gentlemen, together with Charles Day and another pitman, went into the pit. They had not been down long before Mr Spruce returned to fetch blankets, saying that Mr Dugdale had been found, still alive, but badly injured. When the rescuers reached the pit bottom, they found that they could not see at all, and had the greatest difficulty in breathing. They called out and a faint voice had answered. Marsh and Stokes crawled forward on their hands and knees, to find a man lying on his back, a few yards past the point where the Water Level passed underneath the main haulage road. He was dragged, with great difficulty, to the pit bottom and brought to the surface where he was taken into the winding enginehouse, and treated by four doctors who had been standing by.

Repeated attempts were made to find the rest of the missing rescuers, several of them fruitless, but eventually two more were found and brought out. Charles Day was adamant that he had heard a further voice calling. After a tally was taken, it was realised that Rowland Till, a pit carpenter, was missing. A party was organised, including a young miner, a volunteer from Hall End colliery named Charles Chetwynd, who, when they went back into the pit, and despite the thick fumes, crawled on his hands and knees to where it was reported that Till had been heard. He carried a length of rope, which he tied round Till's body and dragged him, barely alive, and shockingly burned, back to the shaft. He died soon after reaching the surface.

Smoke, carbonic acid gas and tar were now coming out of the shafts and the fan. It was decided on Wednesday that no one in the pit could possibly be alive, and anyone trying to enter the pit would be in extreme peril. The only means of containing the fire was by starving it of oxygen, by sealing both shafts six feet below the surface, and also sealing the drift leading to the fan shaft. One of the teams at work sealing the upcast shaft (consisting of Mr Phillips of Ansley, Mr Hardwick, manager of Pooley Hall colliery, Thomas Fretwell and Thomas Walker) were almost overcome by carbonic acid gas. Charles Day was back at the pit, helping with the seals, when the news was brought to him that two of his sons had died of their injuries, and the third son was not expected to live much longer.

Mr Marsh's account

In a letter to a relative, dated June 4th 1882, Mr Marsh gave this account: 'I do not know if you heard of the explosion at a neighbouring colliery, Baxterley the name, but I will tell you of it as it is the first great calamity I have been in.

'The pits were found to be on fire nearly a mile from the surface & still further in were nine men & a boy, who could not get past the fire in consequence of the smoke, so a party of 36 explorers went to find them & help them out, but whilst doing so a terrific explosion of gas occurred, some distance away but the flames completely filled the roads, & there was nothing to breathe but one dense mass of flame, all were horribly scorched & burnt, it was just at this time that I arrived at the pit with the inspector, & we

Hall End
Tamworth.
14 June /82

My Dear Annie,
I feel quite
ashamed of my self for
not writing to you for
so very long a time. I
have had so much trouble
privat + business. that
I am doing so a terrific explosion.
all of gas occurred. Some distance
ha away but the flames completely
e filled the roads. + there was
nothing to breathe but one
dense mass of flame, all
were horribly scorched + burnt—

Mr Marsh's letter.
Copyright Warwickshire County Record Office and
reproduced with kind permission.

volunteered to go down & get them out but just as we were starting down the pit another mass of gas exploded & filled evrywhere with flame but by stuffing our caps in our mouths we managed not to breathe any of it & by burying our faces in our coat sleeves were not burnt except a little hair, so we made another attempt & got out pretty easily 33 of the explorers all alive but terribly burnt nearly all had their eyes burnt quite out & and their tongues were all shrivelled up, we then went down for the remaining three & after going (without lights of course) some 100 yards we stumbled on another man who proved to be the owner of of the mine Mr Dugdale, we got him out & just as we got to the top of the pit there was another explosion, & after waiting for $1/2$ an hour we went down again & in time got out the other two quite dead, so then we knew the nine men & boy could not possibly be alive so we closed them in & and shut up the pit, where they will be for some weeks yet, as well as eleven horses that were burnt, it was the most sickly sight to be imagined my arms were covered with skin and flesh and blood on, & I was completely saturated with blood through carrying the men who in most cases were badly mangled, & felt more like jelly than anything else, all have since died including the owner, Mr Dugdale & two other Mining Engineers & and there does not seem to be a single woman in the whole district round who is not in mourning. We had some very narrow escapes but beyond feeling ill for a week or so from the effect of the afterdamp & a good many small but painfull bruises I for one did not feel much the worse for the adventures, but I shall be boring you so will stop now -'

As the days wore on more and more of the would-be rescuers succumbed of their horrendous injuries and burns, until it reached a total of twenty-three, including Mr Dugdale, plus the original eight men and a boy. It seemed that everyone in the locality had relatives, friends or neighbours, either dead or grievously injured. With the pit sealed off, the 400 men normally employed had lost their source of income. Almost every home's breadwinner had lost his job, and the prospects were grim. A poem was produced, describing the tragedy, and children travelled miles to neighbouring towns and villages, going round door to door selling copies to gain a few pence.

A number of schemes were set up to find work for the unemployed miners. One such was a scheme started by the vicar of Baxterley, the Rev Hugh Bacon, to grow turnips on Baddesley common, known at the time as 'the gold diggings'. For a minimal payment the miners skimmed the turfs off the common and stacked them in rows, and dug the ground between, sowing turnip seed. It was too late in the year to be very successful. The turf banks were still in place until the common was put to the plough during the Second World

War. Only one remains, parallel with Coleshill Road, thirty to forty yards from the road, from the Folly to the 'Top Resser'. Many of the turfs were tipped into the cutting at the entrance to the common tunnel.

Another scheme was building the high wall round the Atherstone side of the Merevale estate, alongside the Coleshill Road and round to opposite the Kings Head pub.

Conditions underground were monitored by removing a plug-in seal on the fan, and checking the contents of the gas issuing from it. It was not until April the following year, 1883, that it was considered safe to unseal the pit, and to proceed to get out the bodies of the night shift originally trapped. Six of the bodies never were recovered, including that of the thirteen year old boy, Joseph Henry Scattergood.

The official Inquiry

One aspect of the affair caused concern at the ensuing enquiry, under the Coal Mines Regulation Act of 1872. Mr Parker, as certificated manager, should have had direct control and supervision of the pit. But he was entirely under the direction of Mr Gillett, who held no certificate, lived at Derby, and visited the pit on rare occasions. He visited the colliery only twice in 1882, the last time only a few days before the incident.

Another concern was that Charles Day, the senior deputy, testified on oath that he had reported the glowing roof coal to Parker on several occasions, although no mention of it was made in his daily reports. As Day was illiterate, he was in the habit of making a verbal report to Parker, who wrote them out for Day to sign. The inquest findings were that 'Mr Gillett and Mr Parker are culpably negligent'. In his report made to Parliament, an MP, Mr Morley, said he could see little difference between the findings of the inquest and of manslaughter. He was most critical of the management of the pit. But the general manager, Mr Pogmore, the manager, Mr Parker, and the mine owner were all killed.

It was decided that the hot flue gases from the boiler had caused burning and baking of the roof coal, producing 'town gas'. This had exploded, causing in turn a number of much larger coal dust explosions. A comparatively small town gas explosion must have happened quite early in the incident, and blown open the air doors, allowing smoke and fumes to get into the intake air roads. Experts considering the affair at the inquiry came to the conclusion that the nine night shift men were probably dead before the alarm was raised.

The ill-fated steam pump was sited immediately below the farm, known as Drybrooks Farm, at the junction of Payne's Lane and the road down Wigston Hill, Baxterley.

Medals and a Relief Fund

All of those who participated in the rescue attempts were presented with a bible and a watch. Some years ago I came into possesion of one of the bibles, and presented it to the Middle School, of which I was at that time a manager.

At a ceremony held at the Corn Exchange, at Atherstone, on Monday February 19th 1883, Lord Leigh, Lord Lieutenant of the county presented Albert Medals awarded by the Queen. First Class (gold) medals went to:

Reuben Smallman, Mining Engineer.
Arthur Henry Stokes, Inspector of Mines
Charles Day, Pit Deputy
Charles Chetwynd, Collier.

Second Class (silver) went to:
Samuel Spruce, Mining Engineer
Frederick Samuel Marsh, Mine Manager
Thomas Harry Mottram, Mine manager
William Morris, Miner
William Pickering, Miner
Joseph Chetwynd, Miner

A relief fund was set up and contributions received from all over the country. The incapacitated and widows received a few shillings a week for life. A copy of a letter is to hand, addressed to the last recipient from the fund, Mrs Clara Ball of Manchester Row, Baddesley, from Richard Fielders, Solicitor:

20th April 1910 .

Madam,

Baddesley Colliery Explosion Relief Fund.

I am directed by the Trustees to send you the enclosed postal order for one pound, 15/- of it being the amount of a small balance which some time ago was allocated for the releif of your late Husband, and 5/- one week's relief due 19th instant. Be good enough to sign and return the enclosed receipt.

The Trustees have decided to pay you five shillings per week until the 31st March 1911 subject to their being satisfied that your case is a deserving one and that the money is properly applied by you. The Trustees reserve the right to withold payment of the relief at any time, should they in their discretion deem it advisable to do so.

Yours truly,

In the 1980s, some of the residue of the fund seems to have found its way to the Warwickshire National Union of Mineworkers at Bedworth. The Merevale Nursing Aid in Sickness Charity then benefitted from it, receiving £720 and £3,000 was given to the Warwickshire Miners Convalescent Fund. Instances have been heard of them issuing sums of ten and twenty, even forty pounds, to local ex-miners as they saw fit.

In May 1932, the tragedy was commemorated by holding a religeous service held in Baddesley. Then, in May 1982, the NCB put on an exhibition at Baddesley Mine to commemorate the centenary.

From Stratford Pit to Baddesley Collieries

One effect of the explosion, when Mr Dugdale died of injuries, was that his oldest son (later to become Sir William Francis Stratford Dugdale) inherited but was eleven years of age, a minor. Trustees were set up to run the mining company, known as Baddesley Collieries Trustees. As the Stratford Pit was the the only colliery, apart from the Speedwell pumping station, the name Stratford became disused. It became known as the Baddesley Collieries, even though it was not in Baddesley but just over the parish boundary in Baxterley. After Nationalisation it became known as the Baddesley Mine.

94

Chapter 6
Post-Explosion Baddesley Pit

The South Staffordshire coalfield had become worked out by this time in the 1870s and all the industries in the Black Country and Birmingham which had been dependant on the coal from South Staffordshire looked for coal from the next-nearest coalfield, Warwickshire. The Warwickshire coalfield was, in one fell swoop, provided with a huge market and lost their most serious competitor. Speedwell, soon followed by Stratford pit, showed the way to get at the coal underneath the wet stratas, and deeper pits were soon being opened all over the Warwickshire coalfield, many with much bigger diameter shafts.

An attempt at Beddesley to develop the Seven Feet seam, on the eastern side of the shafts, came to nothing when when water broke into from the roof in 1884. It was estimated that the inflow was as great as 1,000 gallons [4,000 litres] a minute. The whole of the mine's district had to be sealed off.

In 1896 the output at Baddesley was 400 tons a day, using a two-decked cage in each of the two shafts, but the size of the shafts was the limiting factor. Shortly after that a third fourteen-feet diameter shaft was sunk. It is said that the Dugdale family had to sell works of art to help pay for sinking the third shaft. This was a more modern shaft equipped with steel rope guides, with two double-decked cages, each cage capable of holding four tubs, the two cages passing each other at the mid-point of the shaft. This became No.3 shaft, the two older shafts became known as No.1 and 2 shafts; these became used for ventilation and for manriding.

In the next two decades a number of improvements were carried out on the surface. One large building was erected as a loco shed with a fitting and blacksmiths' shop and a large carpenters' shop (much of the carpentry for the Merevale Estate being done there). During the First World War the fitting shop lathes were used for the production of three-inch shell cases, sent to Russia.

Old Haulage

A large double-drummed, steam haulage engine was installed in a sizable engine house immediately behind the winding engine, and always known as the 'Old Haulage'. It operated two endless steel ropes which traversed the old shafts. One was over a mile long, drawing coal from the 'South Incline' districts; the other was diverted ninety degrees just outside the pit bottom to draw the coal from the 'North Level' districts. It operated the two ropes independently by de-clutching and braking one or other of the drums.

Just after Nationalisation, the north workings became worked out so that only one drum was in operation. It was replaced by a 250 horsepower [187J] electrically-powered haulage engine, installed 300 yards from the bottom of the old shafts.

Introduction of compressed air (piped from surface compressors) provided a means of providing power underground and inbye, being used to operate haulage engines, pumps, coal-cutting machines (which supplanted the tedious and dangerous job of handholing), drills, fans, air picks and numerous other tools, and enabled workings to proceed further and further away from the shafts. The further away from the shafts the workings proceeded the less inclined and less wet the seams became. Compressed air piped from the surface remained in use until around 1950 and was replaced by electrical power. In places where pneumatic tools were called for, such as drilling for blasting purposes when driving roadways through solid rock, then portable electrically-power air compressors were introduced.

The Butty System of payment

After a strike in 1910, the Trustees and Union on behalf of the workmen negotiated a twelve-point Price List, covering every aspect of contract work, the payment for every yard of work and every ton of coal produced. Other conditions set the price to be paid for setting roof supports. The Price List came into force in 1911 and was renewed in 1916, when a second card bearing the twelve points of the Price List was isued to all of the contractors, usually referred to at Baddesley as 'the stallmen'. All coal loaded into tubs was chalked with the stall's number and, when weighed on the surface, was credited to that stall. The company's weighman was accompanied by a checkweighman paid from a fund, known as the 'Checkweigh Fund' subscribed to by all stallmen. The checkweighman was usually the Union Branch Secretary.

The stallman who took a contract for a job, such as a stall, received the payment for the yardage of work done and the tonnage of coal produced, then paid the workmen under them at the day rate for their particular job e.g. handholer, packer, filler or hanger-on, etc. Some of the better-disposed stallmen would pay for their day wage mens' insurance stamp, other did not. Keeping the rest for themselves, the stallmen often received many times as much as their workmen. Giving the underman-ager an orange, nicked with a knife, with a sovereign pushed inside it, or asking if he wanted a match and giving him a box of matches with a pound note folded inside it, were favoured ways of currying favour or ensuring that stallmen retained well-paid jobs. This was known as the 'Butty' system. It was largely replaced when different methods of payment were started at the time that conveyors were introduced.

Clause 10

The Price List was signed on behalf of the workmen by William Johnson, Agent i.e. Warwickshire Miners Union Agent - although 'Cliff' Wood had done most of the negotiating. On behalf of the Trustees it was signed by W.F.S. Dugdale.

The tenth point, always known as 'Clause 10', was of interest. It states: 'In cases of men being fetched away from their work to work on roads or elsewhere, the difference in wages to be made up by the Trustees.' Clause 10 was regularly applied until Nationalisation, when all kinds of changes were made in payments. But, inevetably, a man was taken off his job and claimd Clause 10. The NCB management maintained that Clause 10 no longer applied, but the National Union of Mineworkers backed the workmen and said that it did still apply. As part of the Nationalisation Act catered for a difference between management and union being put before an arbitrator, this was done. The arbitrator found in favour of the workers. So, Clause 10 once more became operative. But it did not end there as workmen in other Warwickshire pits heard about this Clause 10. They claimed also and got the same benefits.

The workers in other areas of the NCB heard, they also successfully claimed. So, until all contract payments were phased out in the 1960s, the NCB operated a nationwide version of Cliff Woods' Clause 10.

An amusing thought. One of Cliff Woods' sons, Albert 'Docker' Wood, was one of the arbitrators appointed for the Warwickshire area. One wonders if he was the one who prolonged the life of Clause 10?

Sankey money

Nationally, the coalowners were believed to have made excess profits during the First World War, as great as 100% profit annually, it was claimed. A Royal Commission under the chairmanship of Lord Sankey investigated the matter. They made a number of recomendations. Each miner was to receive a payment from the excess wartime profits. In addition, a fund was to be set up, to receive $1/_2$d for every ton of coal produced, with the money to be used to improve the welfare of mining communities, through the Miners Welfare Fund. Also, there was a recommendation that the mines should be nationalised. Nothing came of the last recommendation until after the Second World War, but the first two schemes were implemented

The miners received their payment, known as Sankey Money. An unexpected consequence was a blip in the birth rate in mining communities! In Baddesley, the Miners Welfare Fund was instrumental, in conjunction with Baddesley Parish Council, in acquiring a Recreation Ground. The miners from Atherstone benefitted by having a Miners Welfare Club provided.

The 1926 Lock Out and General Strike

In 1925 the coalowners nationally claimed that profits were too low, and demanded that the miners accept a reduction in pay and work half-an-hour longer each day. If the miners did not accede to their demands they would be locked out. The transport and railway unions declared solidarity with the miners, saying that if the miners were locked out, they would call their members to strike in sympathy - a General Strike. The government of the day under Stanley Baldwin made up the miners' wages for a year. But when the miners were locked out in 1926 a general strike started. The miners at some pits yielded to the owners' demands and started working the longer day for less pay. One local pit to

98

do so was Pooley Hall. The whole of the Leicestershire coalfield also complied.

The transport and railway workers strike brought chaos to the country, but after less than a week they returned to work, leaving the miners on their own. They stood out for six months but finally had to yeild.

It was six months of glorious weather, the sun shining almost every day. In Baddesley most of the miners did what they traditionally did in the circumstances, they went 'delving'. Delving was digging, either in old spoil banks, or at the basset of a seam, to find coal to sell to help keep their families. Soup kitchens were set up to provide the children with some food, one on the commom opposite the New School, the other at the entrance to the Parkside, adjacent to the junction with Newlands Road.

There was one unpleasant incident in the village. The men would congregate to 'boo' the few who defied the union's call for solidarity, as they walked home from work. One day a squad of police appeared, with some gentleman, who proceeded to say something that could not be heard in the clamour, presumably it was the Riot Act. The senior police officer present shouted out 'Arrest that man, that man and that man', pointing to three sections of the crowd as he shouted. Wherupon the crowd took to their heels with the police chasing them. Three men were caught and arrested: 'Joey' Sanders, Jim 'Gammy' Chetwynd and my father. My father was arrested in the village street as he was walking along carrying my three-year-old sister. A policeman snatched her out of his arms and arrested him. This was witnessed by Mrs Stokes, who at the subsequent trial testified to that effect, and he was released. The other two each got three months' imprisonment.

Jim Chetwynd was wearing a 'straw boater' hat and it was always believed that he was arrested because of this. William 'Cliff' Wood, President of the Warwickshire miners union and Secretary of the Baddesley branch or lodge, and Tom Smith, an officer of the Baddesley lodge, both were in the habit of wearing boaters. It was thought that they were the ones the police wanted.

Chapter 7

Mining in the 1930s

The 'Pans' or Conveyors

There was a dramatic change in the system of mining at the pit in 1928 when conveyors were introduced. The cost of introducing these was quite high, and because of this the company got rid of some of its older overmen, and replaced them with younger men. The effect on wages was that fillers and packers, who until then had received a bare day wage, now received a wage only a pound-or-so less than the stallmen. A man who had a job on the 'pans' was considered well off. But one contract that did not change was the coal cutters' one, where the chargeman received 60% of the contract himself and his team shared the remaining 40%.

Four 150 yard long faces, each with three gates or roadways, were kept working. As one reached the boundary and was closed another was already prepared ready to start up. This system continued until after Nationalisation in 1947.

Miners Welfare Pithead Baths

March 1931 was a milestone in the lives of the Baddesley miners and their families, with the opening of the pithead baths. For 1d a day the miners could shower and change their clothes before returning home in clean 'shifting' clothes. The housewives lost the chore of having hot water ready for their men folk to wash themselves when they returned home from their shift in the pit. In those days domestic hot water systems were a rarity, in fact unheard of in the ordinary miner's home. The wives had to cope with working clothes or 'pit clothes', soaked in sweat and coal dust, and frequently in sweat and rain. With only one fire, this necessarily fulfilled all purposes - cooking, space heating and drying these 'pit clothes' ready for the next shift. When a wife had a husband and a son or sons working at the pit (especially when they were on different shifts, dayshift, afternoon shift or night shift) she would have her fire guard draped with drying pit clothes for most of the twenty four hours, with the consequential smell of drying sweat and film of coal dust. The 'baths' were as big a boon to the womenfolk as to the men.

Each man had two lockers. Coming off shift he would disrobe, hanging his working clothes in a heated 'dirty locker', then shower, put on his clean clothes from his 'clean locker', before travelling home, by bus, clean and tidy.

The Romans had mines in this country, during their four centuries of occupation. There has been found a copy of their laws relating to the use and maintainence of mine baths - even for the slaves, who also had to bathe after working their shift. It seems strange that only 1,500 years later we managed to copy them.

The Crut

Around 1931 a steeply inclined roadway was driven through the stone, from a 'crut' in the pit bottom, to meet the Two Yard seam, over 1,000 yards inbye from the shaft. It became known as the 'Crut Steep' or simply, 'the Crut'. The Crut provided a haulage road for coal produced on the western side of the workings. Until then, coal had to be hauled well over 1,000 yards eastward to reach the South Incline haulage road, still over 1,000 yards from the pit bottom.

The Crut was driven using 'square work', that is, using straight girders, in the top, bottom and sides at two feet intervals, the whole of it being concreted. It was said at the time that it cost £1 an inch to drive. It was served by a one-and-one-eighth inch endless steel haulage rope, driven by an electrically-powered haulage engine, sited in the engine house of the old steam haulage engine at the bottom of the old shafts.

The Crut created two almost-seperate pits and the western side became known as the 'Crut side' of the pit. It reduced the amount of walking the men had to do in the pit, and increased the length of time they worked. The agreement with the company was that the owners paid for one winding and one walking time, the men did the other winding and walking in their own time. The shorter the walking time the longer the working time. One other advantage was that men working on the Crut side of the pit no longer had to traverse the dreaded 'Incline'.

The Recession

The recession following the Wall Street crash in 1929, when millions were unemployed, together with the iniquitous 'Means Test', was a traumatic period shared by the miners with all the other working people in the country. Baddesley came off better than other local mining communities really, even though almost a half of its workforce was laid off. Baddesley coal being of a higher quality, it was more in demand than other local coals, and so the pit worked more often than did its neighbouring pits. As families tended to be larger in those days, most households had one or two members working even if it was for only three days a week.

A tiny notice about the size of this book would be posted, saying 'the pit will be at play tomorrow'. There was nothing playful to men reading it but, as a fourteen-year old working at the pit, it sounded reasonable - I could spend a day playing with my mates.

Annual Holiday

For the last couple of years before World War II, the miners got a week's holiday with pay. The first week in August the pit closed down for a week. Before this they were only given two days off, Bank Holiday Monday, the statutory holiday (for which they were paid) and the following day.

By this time everyone (except Mr Chamberlain) knew that war was imminent, so that the pit was working full-time. So, many of the men were able, for the first time, to start taking a week's holiday away from home.

The New Power House

Around the same time a new electric generating station was built, complete with six Lancashire steam boilers and a new taller chimney. During the pit's life, up to a dozen chimneys were in use, as the steam generating plant was moved around, probably to accomodate newer more efficient boilers. However, from the position of some of these chimneys, it would seem that some of them were ventilation stacks.

102

World War II

Conscription started in 1939, and a few of the mineworkers over 18 were called up in the Militia, so mining was designated a reserved occupation. Most of the 18- to 20-year old miners who wanted to join the forces when the war did start got around the reserved occupation restriction by joining the Territorial Army. Quite a high percentage of the younger men joined the TA in the first few months of 1939, and were automatically called to the colours when the war did start in August. This shortfall of miners was partly remedied by young men in other occupations, or who were working on the pit surface (an unreserved occupation). Those who wanted to avoid military service could start working underground. Other young men, wishing to serve in the forces, found various ways of getting around the reserved occupation rule. Everyone had to register for National Service, and quite a few men, by not describing their jobs correctly, found themselves 'called up'.

The shortfall in manpower was later made good by the recuitment of 'Bevin Boys', men who registered for National Service, who were directed into the pits instead of the forces. They all left the pits as soon as they were able to.

Pit Air Raid Shelter

An air raid shelter, in the form of a tunnel with two entrances, was driven through the embankment adjacent to the 'Iron Bridge', which crossed Coleshill Road. It was never used as an air raid shelter, but was used after the war as a venue for underground fire fighting training. The single bomb that fell on the pit premises landed only a few yards from the entrance to the air raid shelter. Most of the bomb damage consisted of blown out windows, including most of the glass roof of the Pithead Baths.

War Service

Most of the men at the pit had a second job for the duration of the war. Miners by day and, by night, Air Raid Wardens, Special Policemen, Home Guards, Auxilliary Firemen or any of a variety of other wartime jobs. Many of their wives and daughters, directed into 'munitions', produced war weapons in Coventry and Birmingham. They received double and even treble the wages that their menfolk received from the pits. This was far better than the men in the forces were paid, just 7/- per week (35p in today's currency).

The miners got one benefit. After the war they were sold army ration packs, one to each miner. These were a big help to the men and their families as rationing was still in force. One aspect particularly pleased the men. Cigarettes were difficult to obtain - and each ration pack contained a tin of sixty cigarettes.

Manriding Haulage

Shortly after the outbreak of war, a project that had been worked on for several years came to fruition. The 'Manrider' was opened in the South Return. This transported men for a mile and three quarters into the workings, saving the men an uphill trudge, and giving the owners a longer working day. However it only benifitted the men working on the South side of the pit, the men working on the Crut side had to wait until 1945 when the '8 South Manhaulage' was brought into service.

Chapter 8

Nationalisation of the pits

'Vesting Day' was the day that the newly-formed National Coal Board took over the pits in March 1947. It could not have happened at a better time for Baddesley pit, as it was running out of coal to work. Since the pit came into operation, in 1853, it had mainly been working the Two Yard or (as it was known at the pit) the Ryder Seam. There had been a few places where other seams had been worked, but only on a small scale. By 1947 they had reached their boundaries of the Ryder seam, and were really scratching around after small oddments that had been left. Production was well down. But, as well as the pits being nationalised, minerals were also nationalised. This meant that the old pit boundaries no longer existed. Districts were opened to take coal at Baddesley previously belonging to other neighbouring pits. Production was very soon restored to normal.

The old owners had started to develop other seams some time before. Two steeply-inclined (1:2.8) roadways had been driven from the Ryder seam down to the Bench seam, one each side of the pit. Two larger, less steeply-inclined roadways had also been started, but abandoned. By Vesting Day they were caved-in and flooded. There is little doubt that if the subject of nationalisation had not arisen, the owners would have have had these fully prepared, ready to start production, when the Ryder seam boundaries were reached. A tremendously expensive undertaking that was made unnecessary.

From the outset, during the very first week, the NCB introduced the 'Five Day Week'. This meant that men who worked the five days from Monday to Friday were not expected to work on the Saturday, but were paid for it anyway. But failure to complete the five days disqualified the payment for Saturday.

Apart from the change in management, the greatest change that nationalisation brought was the new equipment - mainly bigger and more-powerful belt drives, haulages, coal cutters etc., instead of the second-hand plant re-used time and time again.

The Panzers

Four or five years after the NCB took over, the Panzerforderer was introduced at Baddesley, one of the first to be introduced in the country. An 'armoured face conveyor' (AFC) of German design and manufacture, which became the basis of all mechanised face equipment. At the time of its installation it was said to be part of Germany's war reparations.

The 'Panzer', as it became known, was manufactured by the Westphalia Mining Company in Germany, and Westphalia engineers came and supervised the installation and trained local men in its use and maintenance. They set a very high standard. All the time that the standards set by the Germans were maintained the wear on the equipment was minimal.

The 'Panzer' was used in conjunction with a Mavor and Coulson 'Sampson Stripper'. This consisted of hardened steel wedges operated by hydraulics, wedging coal off the face on to the Panzer. Baddesley Ryder coal was a high quality 'Household Coal', which meant large coal was very much in demand in those pre-smokeless fuel days. And the Stripper's wedging action produced large coal. In those days large coal was at such a premium, that the NCB appointed a Large Coal Officer (a district appointment) whose job it was to go round the collieries in his take, looking for operations that reduced the sizes of coal being produced.

The Stripper was preceeded down the face by a high-speed, conveyor-mounted middle-dicing coalcutter. This, together with the nine inches of pricking on the floor of the seam, gave the conditions suitable for the Stripper to operate. Several faces were worked-out using the Stripper but, as the coal extraction extended further south (where the coal seams tended to run together) the floor pricking, between the Ryder coal and the Bare coal, disappeared. This made the Stripper ineffective.

The Stripper was replaced by the 70 horsepower [52kJ] floor-mounted Trepanner in the 50s, and in the 60s by the conveyor-mounted Disc Shearers and the Double-Ended Conveyor-Mounted Trepanner. Baddesley was the colliery where this machine was first tried out. The manufacturers, Anderson & Boyes, had technicians based at the pit for some time until it proved itself successful. With the introduction of these coal-getting machines, together with the hydraulically-operated walking chocks, a system known as 'total caving' was brought into use. What this meant was that the method used before - of building packs throughout the face to minimise convergance - was dispensed with, allowing the whole of the 'gough', or in Baddesley's parlance the 'gob', to cave. This further reduced the number of facemen needed.

The 1958 Changeover

The 'change over', as it was known, was when the pit was modernised. This entailed the 14 feet diameter shaft being sunk 600 feet deeper, so the the coal could be transported to the shaft bottom from the two loading points, down a locomotive road employing a slight gradient (1:200) in favour of the load. Previously, coal had to be hauled several hundred yards up haulage roads to the old pit bottom.

There was a severe hiccup. It was planned that 30-cwt [1.5 tonne] mine-cars should be used. All the equipment to handle cars of this size were ordered and much of it delivered to the pit. Then there was a last minute change of mind, to use longer, higher, two-ton minecars. This caused all sorts of troubles, especially in the shaft and in the lower deck of the pit bottom. The higher, longer cars meant that the lower deck had to be made higher, and the longer cars caused problems as rail curves had to be made tighter and more troublesome. The two machines for lowering full cars to the bottom deck and for raising the empty cars from the bottom deck had to be set at a steeper angle than they were designed for, causing unneccessary problems, which persisted throughout the rest of the life of the pit. The slightly larger cages needed to carry the bigger minecars rubbed in the shaft. Whenever the shaft was not in use relays of men were employed chasing the shaft's brickwork, i.e. chiselling part of the brickwork away. Until someone came up with the idea of adjusting the weights hanging on the guide ropes, the guide ropes held the cages in line whilst travelling through the shaft. An innovation was that the weighing office was sited in the pit bottom.

The rope haulages were replaced by electrically-powered locomotives using massive rechargeable batteries, the 15-cwt [750kg] tubs being replaced by mine cars. The preparatory work took several years, but the actual changeover took place during the two weeks annual holiday at the beginning of August 1958. The work underground was completed before the shutdown, but a tremendous amount had to be completed on the surface during those two weeks. The whole of the tub circuit had to be torn out and replaced by a smaller mine car circuit. Underground, the coal was transported from the faces by way of trunk conveyors, right out to two loading points where the mine cars were filled.

This changeover to a more efficient transport system, together with fewer men being employed on the mechanised faces enabled the workforce to be more than halved. This was achieved by older men accepting voluntary redundancy. The Pithead Baths, which a few years before had been enlarged, was made half-empty. The Lamp Room, the Time Office and the Deployment Office were all moved into space made vacant in the Baths.

Underground, another deeper seam, the Bench Seam, was worked, the Seven Foot seam already having been started on. On the south side of the pit two seams ran together forming a thicker seam, known as the Nine Foot. This also was extensively worked later. But the Four Foot seam (although it was proved in a number of places around the pit) was never worked, whereas the Birch Coppice pit sank a shaft especially to work this seam.

Baddesley pit was fortunate in as much that from Vesting Day there was a series of good managers, who improved conditions underground. The pit was prone to heavy weighting, or convergance, and over the years a system of ripping, known as 'systematic ripping', had evolved. The benefits of this system were that the roadways were kept in good condition and supply roads were high enough to enable monorails to be installed in some districts. All coal-bearing belt conveyors were adapted for man-riding, and the roads were kept high enough for full-sized mine cars to travel right up to the faces. The three South Incline trunk conveyor belts, each one approximately 1,000 yards in length, were installed in 1961. They used the belting originally installed for thirteen years, without a belt breaking in the whole of that time, because the joints (the usual place where the belts broke) were replaced systematically and road height enabled friction to be minimised.

The coal-getting machines were constructed in sections to facilitate transport underground (usually consisting of three sections - the haulage section, the electric motor and the disc section, to which the coal-cutting disc was attached). In the 1960s, when a section broke down, the mechanical staff would start parting the machine. The transport system was so good that a new section could be brought from the Central Stores at Ansley, be transported underground, and be on the spot by the time that the machine had been parted ready to receive it.

Most maintenance work was done on a regular systematic basis. The hydraulically-operated haulage sections were replaced at weekends, after a predetermined number of yards of coal had been cut. Over 200 'walking chocks' were installed on a face in a weekend without interrupting production. This was repeated on several faces. In 1961 a more modern, more efficient, electrically-powered winding engine was installed, steam engines being notoriously inefficient. As one manager used to say, 'Keep the pit in good heart, and you can't stop the coal coming'.

During the 1950s a feasibility study was done on replacing the old coal screening plant. Euphamistically named 'The Dry Cleaning Plant', when in use this threw a cloud of dust into the air, invading all the houses in the locality. The study was shelved for a decade, then resurrected. In the meantime the output had increased somewhat, but it would seem that no one thought to update the study. When a new washery plant was built (where the coal and stone were seperated by a floatation process) it was under-capacity. Only with a struggle did it cope with the increased output for the whole of the plant's life.

After a change in management, men were taken off the systematic repairing of the roadways and put to coal production. Production increased, for a time, then the roadways started closing up. When a one disc section of a machine failed, it took two months of roadway repairs before a new section could be transported to replace it. And, whereas before, several 40 gallon [150 litre] barrels of the varying types of oil for the coalface machines used to be transported to the coalfaces on one vehicle, now a man had to crawl up the roadways dragging a couple of gallons of oil in a paper 'packing' bag. Inevitably production suffered.

Around the same time a national policy was introduced, of paying face workers by the shift, instead of them being paid according to the tonnage they produced. In pit jargon, 'contract work pay' was replaced by a 'daywork wage'. This removed the incentive to produce the maximum possible and also had an effect on production. Roadways closed up, conveyor belt roadways became so low and narrow that the belts rubbed on the sides of the roadways, belt breakages became the norm instead of the exception. Supply roads became the same and the greatest difficulty was experienced in transporting supplies. The pit never really recovered from this period. Much later a system of bonuses was introduced, which changed the attitude of the men completely. They worked like Trojans to maintain or increase their bonus.

In the last few years of the pit's life, several totally unnecessary (to the mind of most people at the pit) major projects were implemented. One was when the remaining boilers (which were only used for pit top heating), together with the boiler house and chimney, were demolished to be replaced by a computerised boiler system. The other was when the weighbridges were superceeded by a a system which weighed the railway tankers leaving the mine while they were on the move.

It was alleged that these two projects cost several million pounds each, and that they were put in to put the pit in a bad light, making it look a loss-making mine. The employees of the contractors who put in the boiler system used to say that every pit where they had installed the system had been closed within two years.

Baddesley pit closed in February 1988, after a life of 135 years. Some of the workers, over fifty years of age, received a redundancy payment of up to £38,000, plus a pension until they reached 65 years of age.

Chapter 9

Baddesley Parish Council

Until 1894, the affairs of the Parish were conducted by a Vestry Meeting. The Vestry Meeting consisted of the two Poor Law Overseers, the two Churchwardens and the Vicar, plus the Assistant Poor Law Overseer, who took the minutes and dealt with the day-to-day parish affairs, such as rate collection and dealing with Poor Law affairs. In that year there was an Act passed, that each parish should elect a Parish Council, to replace their Vestry Meetings.

To comply with the Act, a meeting was held at 6.30 p.m., on December 4th 1894, with the object of forming a Parish Council. The Poor Law Overseers, Messrs S. Sprigg and Herbert Wood read the notice convening the meeting, and by common consent the Vicar, the Rev H. Wilson Lee took the chair, at 6.37 p.m.. Thirteen nominations for Councillors were handed in. After an interval of fifteen minutes, the Chairman read Rule 8 pertaining to the questioning of candidates, but no one had any questions. At 7.35 a show-of-hands vote was conducted, but it seemed to be inconclusive, as the Chairman pointed out to the meeting that as only six councillors were called for and, unless the number of candidates was reduced to six, an expensive poll of the village would be necessary.

A general discussion ensued, at the end of which four candidates withdrew their names but the Chairman ruled that, unless three more candidates withdrew their names before the expiration of six days, a poll would be held. The meeting closed at 8.0 p.m.

A further meeting was held on December 20th 1894, when three more of the candidates withdrew their names, this saving the village the expense of an election. The Returning Officer duly named Messrs C. Albrighton, T. Albrighton, Joseph Chetwynd, Arthur Morgan, William Sharrott and William Wood as the appointed body constituting the Parish Council. The Parish Council then held its first meeting, with the Assistant Poor Law Overseer taking the minutes. The Parish Overseer, Herbert Wood, and H. Wilson Lee, the Vicar, sat in on this first meeting. William 'Cliff' Wood was unanimously appointed Chairman and Arthur Morgan appointed Treasurer.

At a meeting held on April 17th 1895, William Wood, more commonly known in the village as 'Cliff' Wood, tendered his resignation as Chairman and Mr George Clamp was appointed in his place. At the same meeting Herbert Wood was re-appointed Poor Law Overseer and Mr Frank Jones, grocer and baker, was appointed Assistant Overseer, with other duties connected with the council. These included the collection of rates in the village, and doling out any Poor Law assistance, often in the form of loaves of bread, for a salary of £12 per year. He had to find surity for himself of £100 and two others of £50 each.

A few years ago I was shown one of the old rate collection books, for the year 1903. Mr Jones' daughters had pasted poems and songs on all of the pages, leaving just two pages still legible. One contains the following declaration:

'We the undersigned do hereby declare that one of us or some person on our behalf has examined and compared the several particulars in the respective columns of the above rate with the Valuation List made under the Authority of the Union Assessment Committee Act 1862 in force in the Parish and the several hereditaments are to the best of our belief rated according to the Valuation appearing in such Valuation Lists and we also declare that the total of the above Rate amounts to one hundred and two pounds seventeen shillings and eleven pence

John Jones
George Dixon
Overseers

The other page was from the list of ratepayers and the amount they paid, the book being one printed especially for the purpose. The list contained 15 names of property occupiers, ten of whom paid 9s 5d [47p], one 8s 0d [40p] and two who paid 5s 10d [29p]. The only two properties mentioned that I can place are the two occupied by two widows, Mrs Margaret Radford and Mrs Bertha Slack, who occupied the houses now No.'s 9 and 11, Newlands Road. Both of these were owned by Mrs Slack; they both paid 9s 5d rates.

William Wood resigned as Chairman of the Parish Council at the April 1895 meeting but, when Mr Clamp resigned from the position due to ill health in 1912, Mr Wood was co-opted back as Chairman and remained Chairman,

White Horse Corner. The chimney pots of the White Horse Inn peep over the cottage roof.

un-elected - being co-opted each term, for nearly forty years. He was also Secretary of the Baddesley Lodge of the Miners Union, President of the Warwickshire Miners Union and a JP. He was the leading figure in starting Baddesley Liberal and Working Mens Club and was the Secretary of the Club for the first forty years of its existence.

Another of the village stalwarts, and a close friend of Cliff Woods, was Mr Tom Smith. When Frank Jones resigned from the post of Assistant Poor Law Overseer, a post which changed its title later to Clerk to the Parish Council, Tom Smith resigned from the Parish Council to take over the post, and held it until after World War II. He was also Treasurer of the Miners Union Lodge and Treasurer of the Liberal Club from its start until 1948.

At their third meeting the Parish Council decided to find out whether there was any demand for allotments (supplying parishioners with allotments being one of the duties of a Parish Council). They decided to ask Mr Sprigg, a farmer, if they could rent part of the field known as Beggars Barn Close for use as allotments by the parishioners living in the upper part of the village. And to ask Mr William ('Billy') Wood, a farmer of Baxterley, if they could have the use of part of the field adjacent to Baddesley Wood, opposite Mr Thomas Whittaker's, for allotments for the residents of Lower Baddesley.

113

It is also on record that they tried to rent the New Building Close for use as a recreation ground, but the Minute Book states that no one would 'advocate for' the field at the terms offered. There were two football teams in the village at this time, the Wesleyans and the Congregationists or 'the Congs'. They had to go outside the parish to play home matches, through Grendon Wood to the two fields on the Grendon side of the wood. One team played in the field on the right hand side of the road, the other team played in the field on the left hand side. There are very few fields in Baddesley that are on the level, hence the trek through Grendon Wood to play matches. The field on the right hand side was a hive of activity during and just after the World War II, as it was the site of Sir Alfred McAlpine's headquarters when his firm were extracting coal from Grendon Wood. The field contained the offices, fitting shop, stores, canteen, garages, etc., and was on-the-go twenty four hours a day.

There were a number of changes the Parish Council tried to make for the village. They tried to get gas laid on to the village. This was a long running thing - the Councillors had been trying to get this done from the time that the Parish Council was set up. The last time they asked for it they conducted a survey to find how many residents would change to gas and, even though a national gas main passed right through the parish (two 36 inch [1m] pipelines pass under the viaduct), they received an outright refusal to their request. Then, suddenly, two years later British Gas suggested laying gas around the village, claiming that new technology had made it a viable proposition.

The Parish Council asked the railway to run a train for shoppers from Atherstone to Baxterley. And asked the doctors to organise a calling office in Baddesley to save the sick people having to walk to Atherstone to see a doctor. One thing they succeeded in doing was to have a polling station in Baddesley. They complained that Baddesley residents, having to walk up Bentley Hill to Bentley School to cast their votes at elections (a two mile walk up the steepest hill in the locality) was, in their view, inconvenient.

Nicknames

Mentioning 'Cliff' Wood brings to mind the Baddesley nicknames. Almost everyone in the village had a nickname. Some were of neccessity, as when there were five Jack Fretwells, four Arthur Chetwynds and so on. But there were family nicknames also. The ones that spring most readily to mind are the Albrightons. There were the 'Wakey' Albrightons, the

Yew Tree Cottage, in Newlands Road.
This used to be the Old Black Horse Inn.

'Stumpy' Albrightons, the 'Kitty' Albrightons, the 'Toddy' Albrightons, the 'Dergin' Albrightons, the 'Cob' Albrightons, the 'Dessy' Albrightons, the 'Jainter' Albrightons and the 'Buttoney' Albrightons - plus a family of Albrightons to whom no nickname was attached.

With some of the families, for instance the 'Stumpys' and the 'Dergins', the nickname could be traced back to the grandad. But in the case of the 'Wakeys' the origin of this nickname is lost in the mists of time, and often it would be difficult to trace the relationship between one 'Wakey' and another. One man named Frank Albrighton had the nickname of 'Codger', and as he was a 'Wakey' Albrighton, he was 'Codger Wakey' instead of Frank Albrighton. Bear in mind however, that there were two other Frank Albrightons in the village at the time.

Parkside Road

In 1900, the Baddesley Colliery Trustees, without consultation or forewarning, closed what had until then been the main road from Baddesley to Baxterley, the Parkside. The Trustees put a gate at the point where the road passed from Baddesley Common to Baxterley Common. The Parish Council reacted most strongly and claimed that, as the Dugdales had not closed the road when they enclosed Baxterley Common (thirty-odd years before), they had no rights to close it. It did no good, the road remained closed. The

Another Yew Tree Cottage, also in Newlands Road. This was demolished in 1962; the site is now the entrance to Meadows Gardens.

Trustees surfaced Rotherhams Hill as a substitute, but that was never fenced or adopted as a road by the Highway Authority and has declined since to a bridle path.

Mains Water

Mains water was laid around the village in 1902. Not to each individual house but to a few street taps which were cast iron cylindrical devices, approximately three feet high with a domed top and a lion's face on the front. When a knurled knob in the position of the lion's left ear was turned, water came out of the beast's mouth. Householders now fetched water from the street taps, instead of from the wells as they had to previously. Despite the fact that the village is on top of a hill the water table is not far below the surface; in many cases a house or row of houses would have a well in the garden.

The principal wells had been: Town Well in the fields off Holly Lane; the Waterloo Well which was sited opposite Church House (this was the shaft of the old Waterloo Pit, of 1815, which was never filled in but left to form a water well, eventually being capped after the mains water was laid on); the other well of note was Tomtits Well on the common, opposite Allens Row.

116

Tomtits Well supplied Allens Row with water, and later with water for their gardens. It was a shaded well, having a cap stone, to shade the water and prevent algae forming on it. Not until children or youths tipped the cap stone over from the well, after Allens Row was demolished, was it was realised that the capstone was one of the millstones from the old mill on Mill Knob.

One of the few houses to be supplied with water right up to the house was the Vicarage. This had a lead pipe delivering water to a tap in the yard outside the kitchen door. Yet we find that the Vicar complained to the Rural District Council that the Vicarage had a dead-ended lead pipe feeding it. This did not get him very far, however. The Chairman of the Parish Council said, 'He'll be treated the same as everyone else'.

Baddesley Parish Council paid for the pipes to be laid to supply both the 'Rookery', at Baxterley, and upper Grendon. Later, when the New Sinkings Pit was sunk, an agreement was reached between Morris and Shaw, owners of Birch Coppice pit, and Baddesley Parish Council, for pipes to be laid and to supply the new pit with water. This was often called the Wood End Pit, but was actually in the parish of Baddesley.

The Parish Council had already laid pipes to supply Baddesley Farm and other farms a little lower down the Lower House Lane. The water to supply the local mains was pumped from behind the tubbing of the shafts at Stratford Pits (where the shafts passed through the water bearing stratas) to a water treament works at the top of Bentley Hill. This gave the supply the 'head' needed to push the water everywhere it was needed. But the water was very 'hard', containing a lot of gypsum, making all vessels used for boiling it prone to furring up, and also making the water difficult to lather, so that it took a lot of soap or soap powder to use it for laundering. Every house had a water butt or cistern to catch the 'softer' rain water, for use on wash-day. Soft water remained at a premium until detergents were introduced in the 1950s.

Sewage Field

The first mention of the sewage field, or 'Sock Field', as it was known in the village, was in the *Atherstone Express* of September 5th 1907. An article reported that a Baxterley farmer, Mr 'Billy' Wood, was sub-letting a plot of ground three to four acres [approx. 1.5 hectares] in extent for £45 a year to Baddesley Parish Council for use as a sewage field. The proper rent for a plot of that size was a fifth of that amount. There is no mention of the sewage field in the Parish Minutes until March 1915, when they decided to 'adopt the scheme', by buying the sewage field (eight and a half acres [3.4 hectares] in extent) by mortgage.

The Rural District Council took over the field when they became responsible for sewage in the early 1920s. It seemed ironical that the Parish Council should have to rent part of the field they bought in 1915, when in the early 1970s they wanted more land for use as allotments. The field was no longer used for sewage purposes by that time, a sewage scheme having been introduced. By way of a large bore pipe, Baddesley and Baxterley sewage is delivered to a larger sewage works built at Grendon. This follows the course of the Sugar Brook and the Penmire Brook, then via Speedwell, under the viaduct, alongside the old churchyard, and passing under the Watling Street alongside Whites Farm, Grendon.

Electric Power

From the time that the Parish Council was formed they had been trying to get gas into the village to light the homes of the parishioners. By 1924 electricity was beginning to appear. A local pit, Pooley Hall, was producing electricity to power its underground plant, then went one further and supplied local communities with electricity for domestic lighting. Arrangements were made with Pooley to supply Baddesley and, in the next couple of years, each house in the village was equipped to take four five-amp light fittings. Before this the only domestic lighting available in the village had been candles and parafin oil lamps. Many shops sold parafin for lamps, besides which traders came around the village, especially on Friday evenings and Saturdays, with their horse-drawn drays carrying large tanks of parafin for sale.

There was an exception. When in 1916 the Liberal and Working Mens Club built their first purpose-built clubhouse, now the bar at the club, they incorporated an electric generator. So that the Club was lit by electric lights long before the rest of the village.

Domestic electric lighting having been installed to everyone's satisfaction, the Parish Council entered into an agreement with Pooley Hall Colliery to have thirteen street lamps installed. On September 30th 1927 was an official switching-on ceremony. The system was opened by Colonel Chaytor, the proprietor of Pooley Hall Colliery, and the lights were switched on by William Wood JP, Chairman of the Parish Council.

118

Representatives were present of both the Rural District Council and the Grendon Parish Council, with suitable refreshments laid on at the Red Lion Inn. But there was a sting attached. The R.D.C. took over the responsibility for street lighting, so thirty years after Baddesley had installed its original thirteen street lamps, it had to wait until every other village in the district had been provided with a modern street lighting system, before it too was considered for one.

The War Memorial

This did not start out as a Parish Council venture but it finished up as one. In 1919 a general meeting was held to decide whether the village should have a war memorial. The Vicar, Parson Lee (Rev H. Wilson Lee), took the chair. Yes, it was agreed that the village should have a war memorial. Then came the question, 'What form should the memorial take?' There were parishioners present from most organisations in the parish, and a number of propositions were made. The one that carried was that each place of worship in the parish should have tablet installed, bearing the names of the fallen. Also, a clock should be installed in the church tower.

Various people present undertook money-raising activities. Some were personal efforts - for instance, Mrs Florence Fretwell took on the task of a door-to-door collection, and Dick Ball, with the assistance of Miss Wilson Lee, was to organise a tennis afternoon on the vicarage tennis courts. Various groups took on other fund-raising schemes and money started coming in.

The Vicar ordered a clock from John Smith & Son of Derby. This was duly delivered to the Atherstone railway station, and collected from there by Mr Jody Wood, with his horse and cart. It was installed and put to work on July 6th 1920. But at the next meeting of the committee, the news that all the money raised so far had been spent on the clock, and even that was not paid for, did not go down too well. In fact, the committee became a stormy one and disintegrated, with no minutes being taken.

A group of the younger men of the village took on the erection of a granite obelisk, bearing the names of the fallen, by voluntary labour. This was erected on the old dirt mound of the Maypole Pit, opposite to the Maypole Inn. Its plinth is the one currently in use as a base for the Pit Wheel memorial.

In 1933 there were still bills relating to the memorials which had not been paid. After some negotiation, it was decided that the Parochial Church

*The gate on the left was the entrance to the Tater Close, now
Jean Street. The cottages have been replaced by old peoples'
bungalows although the trees are still standing.*

Council should undertake trusteeship of the clock (but the Parish Council pays
for its annual overhaul). The Parish Council would undertake responsibility for,
and trusteeship of, the obelisk. Its plinth was surrounded by concrete posts
bearing heavy ornamental chain. The Government's wartime order that scrap
dealers could take any decorative ironwork led to the chain being burned off
and taken for wartime use. In the same way that the Liberal Clubs' beautiful
wrought iron railings and gates were taken, but many would say stolen was a
better word.

Came the end of the Second World War, and people's thoughts turned to
up-dating the war memorial, adding to the obelisk the names of the five
Baddesley men who lost their lives in the armed forces during the war. This
would entail the obelisk being taken away to be worked on. The most attractive
suggestion was that permission should be acquired to convert the top of the
mound, on which the obelisk stood, into a Garden of Remembrance. The
obelisk then to be put back in the same place. Nothing came of that idea. Fears
of vandalism or abuse led to the obelisk being removed to the churchyard,
where it stands today.

Recreation Ground

The Recreation Ground or, as it has always been known, the 'Rec', was the product of a joint venture between the Miners Welfare Scheme and the Parish Council, with William 'Cliff' Wood and Tom Smith officials in both camps. The Cow Pasture and an adjacent field were bought for £380 and the dividing hedge grubbed out. This entailed several trees being felled and their roots were blasted out by a shotfirer from the pit. A partly-successful attempt was made to level the football pitch, and the tennis court was levelled. In 1924 the Parish Council entered into negotiations about the management of the ground, so a Parks Committee was set up with representatives from the Parish Council, the lodge of the Union and the pit management, with the pit supplying a full-time groundsman. The children's play equipment, swings and such were chained up by him at sunset every evening.

Everything went wonderfully well. The football pitch, cricket pitch and tennis courts were in regular use. Athletic meetings were held there and various village organisations held gala days. One of the highlights of the Rec's year was the cricket match against Warwickshire Cricket Club's Club and Ground team. Many of the county's first team would show up, and Baddesley would invite many really good cricketers to play for them. One year they fielded members of the West Indian national team.

In the 1950s the Parks Committee decided to level the ground out more. They closed the ground and made a start but their plans went a-wry. At the end of the day they had to ask the Coal Industry Social Welfare Organisation (set up on nationalisation to replace the old Miners Welfare Scheme) to step in. They did so, completing the levelling work and building a new brick pavillion to replace the old wooden one. But things were never the same, the village never had a cricket team to use the re-arranged ground. This was partly because the cricket square was encroached upon by a football pitch. After a change of management at the pit, the caretaker was withdrawn, resulting in increased vandalism. Then the management wanted to be rid of any responsibility for the 'Rec' and, in 1980, through the Charity Commissioners the 'Rec' was handed to the Parish Council. But the terms of reference from the Charity Commissioners were that it should be run by a committee, and any and every village organisation who wished to do so could nominate some of its members to

121

the 'Rec' committee. But the way it works out in practice is that it is difficult to get anyone to serve on the committee.

One of the most time-consuming activities the Parish Council has undertaken was the registration of the common, very much to the heart of the vast majority of the parishioners. But this has been dealt with elsewhere.

Doctors in the Village

The Parish Council was, right from the beginning, concerned about health matters in the village. In 1903 the Chairman thanked a Mr J-- (the name is illegible) for his tenderness and care in the recent scarlet fever outbreak. To visit a doctor the parishioners had to walk to Atherstone. The Parish Council approached the local doctors' practice to see if a calling office could be established in the village. The doctors were not at all helpful, suggesting that one be set up somewhere near the Boot Inn (it should be pointed out that, until a few years before that, the only houses on the Watling Street were the ones at Lower Baddesley, the rest have all been built since that time, and there was only one house in Spon Lane. So that the Grendon as we know it today did not exist). Nothing came of it all.

In 1924 the Council managed to get the doctors' practice to agree to use the home of a widowed lady, Mrs Hannah Garratt, as a calling office. She lived opposite the Infants' School, and each of the three doctors in the practice attended there one morning each week, so that the 'calling office' was in use three mornings a week.

Mrs Garratt also got prescriptions made up and delivered to the village. A patient would leave their prescription plus three pence, with Mrs Garratt. She would get Mrs Alice Waite to take them in her horse and cart to the chemist's at Atherstone, get them made up and return the medicaments to Mrs Garratt, ready for the patients to collect in the afternoon. Later, taking the prescriptions to the chemists' and returning the medicines was undertaken by the Evans brothers' De Luxe coaches. The bus drivers picked up the prescriptions and delivered them to the chemist's, then collected the medicaments from the chemists and delivered them to Mrs Garratt's for distribution. Mrs Garratt continued to provide this service for around forty years. The patients would wait their turn to see the doctor in Mrs Garratt's living room, her front room having been converted into a doctor's consulting room.

The health of the community suffered in the twenties and early thirties, especially among the children, due to malnutrition, resulting from the shortage of cash, low wages and shortage of work. Children suffered from diseases one never hears of today, things like rickets. Children suffering from this usually wore leg irons, presumably to keep their legs straight. Then there was the periodical outbreaks of diptheria and scarlet fever. The sufferers were taken to the Isolation Hospital at Archer's Hill, Grendon. The most feared disease was consumption or tubercolosis. This struck down not only individuals but nearly whole families. Sturdy athletic young men succumbed to it. Some lingered on for two or perhaps three years. They would live in a shed in the garden, to avoid passing the germs on to other members of their families, the germs being breath bourne. Also, it was said that fresh air was one of the few ways of countering the disease.

Before the National Health Service was introduced by Nye Bevan in 1948 one had to be a member of a doctor's club to be able to see the doctor. Miners paid to both Hospital and Doctors clubs out of their wages.

Baddesley grew in the forty years Mrs Garratt provided this service. But they were no longer the long-suffering, docile people they had been forty years before, but the recipients of the new free Health Service. The days had gone when they were expected to walk with teenage sons and daughters pushing wheelbarrows or old prams to Mrs Garratts - the wheelbarrow or pram to be used to wheel their children back home, still unconsious from chloroform, having had their tonsils taken out.

Mrs Garratt's cottage became too small for the numbers waiting to see the doctor. The County Councillor, Mrs Allard, intended to get something better and took up the cudgels on behalf of the parishioners. She wrote a letter which was published by the local press. It took nearly a whole page, wading in to the doctors' practice for the facilities they provided at Baddesley. The doctors' reply was to stop using Mrs Garratt's. Anyone wishing to see a doctor had to go to their surgery at Atherstone.

In the meantime, a purpose-built surgery was being put up as part of the community centre in Hunters Park, a matter of fifty yards from the old calling office, at the request of one of the parish's two Rural District Councillors. Which left the village in the ridiculous position of having a purpose-built surgery which was unused. It is sometimes said that it was not much effort to catch a bus to Atherstone or, in the case of car owners, jumping into their car. But it is less easy to do this when one is ill, then (on any day other than Tuesday or Friday) waiting for an hour or so for a bus back.

The Parish Council tried several times to get a doctor to use the surgery, but failed. Then, suddenly in 1988, nineteen years after the surgery was built, having stood empty all that time, a doctor moved in and set up a practice. He applied for permission to dispense his own prescriptions. The application needed to be endorsed by the Parish Council, and the endorsement was to be returned before the next Parish Council meeting. As Chairman, I was the only one empowered to act and was pleased to be in a position to help. I could see no point in prescriptions being issued in Baddesley, and having to be taken to the chemists at Atherstone, to be made up. I endorsed the application, and reported my action to the next Parish Council meeting.

Parish Midwife

For over forty years prior to the introduction of the National Health Service, Mrs 'Ginny' Higgs was the midwife. She lived at 'The Stocks', at Higgs' Corner, known as such for obvious reasons. Most of the senior citizens of the village were brought into the world by her. The job called for travelling to all parts of the village at all sorts of hours of the day and night, but she was a sturdy lady and one would have to be a very brave man to accost her on her travels in the lonelier parts of the village. As children, when we asked where babies came from, one of the more common responses was 'under the gooseberry bush'. I recall a group of us tip-toeing past Higgs' garden, when Mr Higgs was tending his gooseberries.

In the late twenties, another midwife appeared on the scene. She was Nurse Boonham, who lived at Baxterley and travelled round in a small Austin Seven car, one of the few cars seen in the village. She attended the members of the Merevale Nursing Association, who paid a few coppers a week to voluntary collectors. The National Health Service of 1948 brought State Regisered nurses, paid by the state. The funds of the Merevale Nursing Association were utilised in purchasing the house of the old school headmaster which became the residence of the local nurse, until the Warwickshire Health Authority took the nurse away from the village in the 1950s. Now the house stood empty and the Nursing Association, still the owners, sold it. Some years later, ladies of the village started asking what had happened to the funds, and it was found that the Treasurer still held them.

Merevale Aid in Sickness

It was decided that the assets should be utilised to start a charity to be known as the Merevale Aid in Sickness Charity. This would provide sick people with assistance in ways that could not be provided by the Health Service, and to provide surgical appliances in cases of emergency. The charity was administered by a committee, comprising representatives of the four involved parish councils, and members appointed by the committee itself. A sizeable donation was made to the charity from the Explosion Fund, and the Sally Ball Charity's funds became so low that it was considered sensible that the two should merge.

Currently wheelchairs, commodes etc, are held at Penmire Close centre, Hunters Park centre, and at Baxterley for the use of sudden cases of illness, etc. It would be worthwhile for parishioners of the four parishes to know their representatives, in case they ever need help from this charity.

Baddesley now

History is the study of old documents and today more and more old documents are coming available. In the last few years it has been possible to learn more of the Baddesley of the past than was ever possible before. It has not been a case of what I should put in this book so much as what I can leave out while trying to make it readable and informative.

The last pit has closed, the only industry in the parish is the Willprint works, which employs two people, and the sheepskin farm which employs a few. Most of the over-fifties were awarded a pension when they were made redundant. Almost all of the under-fifties have found employment, many of them travelling many miles to and from work.

Nevertheless, at the time of writing, an old friend Mr Tom King has applied to open a drift mine near Colliery Farm, Merivale - that is, just outside the old pit's surface area. He proposes to work the bottom Bench Seam in a drift mine, probably following the seam down from the basset. The Bench Seam consists of two approximately five feet thick seams of fairly high quality coal, parted by twelve to eighteen inches of pipe clay.

So, now Baddesley is purely residential. But its eighty-plus acre common has magnificent views over Leicestershire, Derbyshire, Staffordshire and - if one looks to the west - over Birmingham to the hills the other side of Brum. My opinion is that over the forthcoming years Baddesley will become increasingly 'up market'.

The new village hall encouraged the start-up of a theatrical society - BATS, Baddesley Amateur Theatrical Society - and a pantomime society calling themselves 'The Rockers'. With the coming of the new vicar, Keith Hodson, the church and the chapels are working more closely together than ever before and the community spirit is better than ever before.

Appendix:

Baddesley Ensor field names

The latest map of the parish giving a complete list of the field names is from 1848 by John Dumolo. The numbers relate to the field names given by Dumolo, although these not still in use. Despite the fact that the railway was not opened until 1878, the line has been superimposed to give bearings. The modern street and lane maps have also been added to help the readers locate themselves.

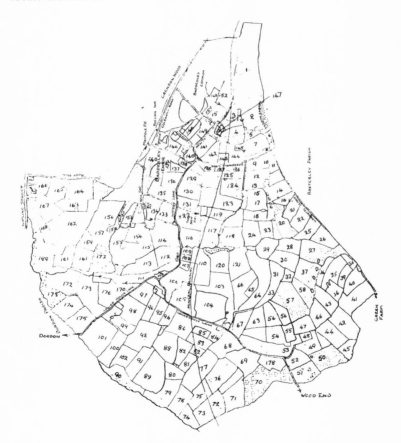

127

1: Part of Baxterley Park
2: Cook's Close
3: Croft, rickyard, orchard and garden
4: Baddesley Close
5: Baddesley meadow
6: Wet Bits
7: Lower Waldron
8: Tillie's Pieces
9: Long Close
10: Nether Top Close
11: Further Top Close
12: Long Days
13: Tillie's Pieces
14: The Moor Close
15: The Long Close
16: The Moor Close
17: Great Barn Close
18: Little Barn Close
19: The Woods
20: The White Wood
21: The Moor Meadow
22: Hovel Close
23: Little Wood Piece
24: Maple Tree Close
25: Crabtree Field
26: Butcher's Close
27: Big Rough
28: Far Friday Field
29: Near Friday Field
30: Ley Reason
31: Little Irons Croft
32: Little Irons Croft
33: Over and Lower Middle Close
34: Piece at the top of the Big Wood
35: The Red Hill
36: Barn Croft
37: The Big Rough
38: Lime Kiln Close
39: Thistley Close

40: Thistley Close
41: Milky Close and Road
42: Far Kings Close
43: Stone Pit Close
44: First Kings Close
45: Little Kings Close
46: Far Over Ridding
47: First Over Ridding
48: House Close
49: Newnes Close
50: Pittams Wood
51: Wood Close
52: Gorse Close
53: Collins Close
54: Spring Close
55: Garden Close
56: Laurance's Meadow
57: Lower Ridding
58: The Little Wood
59: Home Meadow
60: High Meadow
61: Hemp Yard
62: Corner Close
63: Bottom Close
64: The Long Close
65: Collins Close
66: Willingtons Close
67: The Big Croft
68: Ash Flat
69: Over Waste
70: Biddles Rough
71: Upper Waste.
72: Lower Waste
73: Lower Waste
74: Second Lower Waste
75: First Lower Waste
76: Middle Waste
77: Long Stocking
78: Short Stocking

79: Meadow Leys
80: Wood Close
81: Plantation
82: Sweetmore
83: Hungry Hill
84: Orchard
85: Part of Hungry Hill
86: Upper Park Field
87: Wheatmow
88: Nether Park Field
89: The Big Close
90: Meadow
91: Calves Croft
92: Crab Tree Close
93: The Little Park
94: The Little Park
95: Large Park
96: Long Close
97: The Piece
98: Kettle Croft
99: Long Leys
100: Long Close
101: Cow Close
102: Broomy Flat
103: Field Piece and Long Leys
104: Brook Field
105: Peas Croft
106: Normans Croft
107: Large Brook Field
108: Little Brook Field
109: Brook Meadow
110: Pipers Moor
111: Long Meadow
112: Upper Keys Close
113: Lower Tinkers Hill
114: House Close
115: Spring House
116: New Town Close
117: The Far Hill

118: Great Rye Croft
119: The Long Close
120: Calves Croft
121: Lower Willingtons Close
122: Middle Hill
123: Great Barn Close
124: Colins Croft
125: Big Heath Piece
126: Lower Field Piece
127: Middle Field Piece
128: Upper Field Piece
129: Tilley's Close
130: Little Barn Close
131: Far Croft
132: The Golden Croft
133: Upper Tinker' Hill
134: Bye Pit Field
135: Common Close
136: Top Croft
137: New Croft
138: Well Croft
139: Top Croft
140: The Slang
141: Bakers Croft
142: Pratts Piece
143: White Clover
144: Upper Flat
145: Lower Flat
146: Croft
147: Cottage and garden
148: Allens Row gardens
149: Hunters Piece
150: Barn Close
151: Meadow Gardens
152: The Newlands
153: Engine Field
154: Brick Kiln Piece
155: Church Close
156: Over Stocking